Born Contemplative

Born Contemplative

*Introducing Children
to Christian Meditation*

MADELEINE SIMON

DARTON · LONGMAN + TODD

First published in 1993 by
Darton, Longman and Todd Ltd
1 Spencer Court
140–142 Wandsworth High Street
London SW18 4JJ

ISBN 0–232–51990–0

A catalogue record for this book is available
from the British Library

Cover: Jeremy Dixon

Phototypeset by Intype, London
Printed and bound in Great Britain
at the University Press, Cambridge

To all the children of the world
their parents
and their other educators

Contents

Introduction

> Biblical revelation implies an encounter with the Inaccessible and establishes a relationship (a covenant) with him who is essentially Alone. To the human mind this is sheer nonsense.[1]

It is with this 'sheer nonsense' that this book deals. And further, it deals with it in the context of children. To the adult mind the marrying of encounter with inaccessibility, and relationship with aloneness, makes nonsense because it does not come within the reasoning of human logic. Hence, an insurmountable stumbling block. Paul speaks of this same stumbling block when preaching a crucified Christ to the Corinthians: 'To the Jews an obstacle that they cannot get over, to the pagans madness.'[2]

He is preaching a truth beyond the capacity of human reason to capture, a truth that appeared as utter nonsense to those brought up on Greek philosophy, founded on the supremacy of human reason. Moreover, Paul tells them that he has avoided dealing with arguments from philosophy: 'I did this so that your faith should not depend on human philosophy but on the power of God.'[3]

Here we are today, twenty centuries later, faced with the same challenge to our own Christian commitment. We tend to confine our relationship with God to a way which our human reason can capture, thus we need that teaching

1

of Paul every bit as much as did those people of Corinth. Our commitment is not to rest on human philosophy but on the power of God in the darkness of faith.

We learn much about this resting on the power of God in the darkness of faith from *The Cloud of Unknowing*. The author equates the word 'darkness' with 'lack of knowing', and he tells us that, although we can use our minds on all other matters 'yet of God himself can no man think. . . . By love he can be caught and held, but by thinking never.'

The form of meditation discussed in this book is one in which the mind is kept in silence within the darkness of faith through the repetition of a prayer word or mantra. Adults tend to have questions and queries when coming to this form of prayer for the first time, but small children have no such problems. They take to it like ducks to water. They have not reached the stage of logical thought and are able, in their simplicity, to catch and hold God by love.

Born Contemplative is written for adults who are concerned with, and involved in, the religious education of children from their beginnings to around the age of twelve.

The book is primarily for parents and teachers who are themselves practising this form of Christian meditation and who long to introduce it to their children but are hesitant about doing so because they are not sure how to proceed. It could also be used as an appetiser for those who are not yet meditating but would like to learn about it for themselves and for the children in their care. Such people will not find a full initiation in this book but it will put them on their way, and offer them sources of information. It is also hoped that some people who, on picking up the book, have no intention of meditating themselves, will be moved to do so in the interests of their children. Meditation is so simple, so unthreatening and peace-giving.

Some empirically based theology and child psychology will be found running through the pages. This is not a text book in either subject but they are there to ensure that the teaching is sound theologically and that the child feels free enough and loved enough to assimilate that teaching.

Stress is laid throughout the book on the importance of sustaining a positive attitude towards each child in order for the potential within to develop and find expression. 'Never presume to teach anyone anything until you have first learnt something from them' is a piece of advice which applies as much to the teaching of children as of adults. Children have so much to give us if we will but look and listen!

A complete syllabus of religious education will not be found in this book, nor does it provide the schema for a series of lessons for the various age groups. Were it to do so, the initiative would be wrested from the readers. However, a few examples of lessons are given to illustrate the point being made and to act as a guide and an encouragement to parents and less experienced teachers.

It will be noticed that there is a strong emphasis in the book towards the youngest children. This is for the very good reason that these earliest years are, without doubt, the most important and formative time of life. It is also the time when children are solely in the care of their parents or other significant adults, and these are less likely to have had the same training and experience as the qualified teachers of the school years. Further, the general principles of learning and teaching do not change and only need to be related by the teachers to the needs and development of the older age groups.

The opening chapter gives an overall view of meditation, the meaning of the word, the different forms there are and, in particular, the form which uses a prayer word throughout the time of the meditation. Such meditation is seen to have been part of the Desert and Hesychast tradition, and also that of *The Cloud of Unknowing*, and it has come through to a great revival in the twentieth century. The teaching of John Main (1926–82) has played a large part in this revival and it is that teaching which is being related to the leading of children into contemplative prayer in this book.

The second chapter leads on from discussion of the meaning of meditation in itself and applies it to our own lives, discovering in Paul's writings what he means by living in Christ and passing on the Way which Christ taught and embodied. This is a very important chapter and needs to be returned to a number of times. We cannot lead children into meditation with any integrity unless it is grounded in our own lives and we are striving, however inadequately, to follow the Way ourselves.

Chapters 3–4 are of a practical nature. They deal with a mother's attitude during her pregnancy and the first years of her baby's life. The role of the home is talked about together with some practical suggestions as to the integration of meditation with the daily life of the home.

Having spoken of meditation in itself and as applied to our own lives, and then having put it in the context of the home environment, Chapters 5–7 relate it to the lives of the children themselves as they grow from babyhood through to adolescence. We look at the two great themes of Wonder and Scripture, which can lead us powerfully to an ever-deepening relationship with God.

Wonder is the subject of Chapter 5 which discusses how children can be led into an awareness of the breathtaking wonders of the universe by a nurturing of their own inborn gift of wonder. Art and the natural world play a crucial part in this nurturing.

In Chapter 6, before embarking on the teaching of Scripture in Chapter 7, we first address the question of who Jesus is? It is exceedingly important that we distinguish, in our teaching, between Jesus as he was during the 30 years or so that he spent in Palestine before his death, and the risen, post-resurrection Jesus who has guaranteed us his presence for all time. This is the Jesus to whom we relate here and now, but before we can have a loving relationship with him we must come to know him through studying his life in Palestine twenty centuries ago.

This link between the Gospels and our relationship to Jesus in our own lives is discussed in Chapter 7 and a number of lessons to be used with children of varying ages are included as a guide to those involved in leading children into the way of prayer which we call meditation.

The two concluding chapters do not expressly deal with meditation. Chapter 8 gives some information about the culture which influenced the religious formation of Jesus first as a child and then in his life and teaching. There is much that we can learn for our own situation from even such a slight study as this. Finally, in Chapter 9, we take an overview of how children learnt about the faith of their parents in the Early Church, and we reflect on how the Spirit of God is ever at work in amongst all the obstacles within and outside the Church from the time of Jesus' earthly life till now. The parable of the wheat and the weeds growing up together till the end of time gives witness to the fact that Jesus was well aware of this. He has also said that he will be with us till the end of time. He is the wheat eternally springing up in our own lives to be given for others. Take and eat.

I wish to thank all those who have shared their lives with me in the preparation of this book. Special mention must be made of my own religious community, the Society of the Sacred Heart, and of the community here at the Christian Meditation Centre in Royston over the last few years who have borne with me patiently and given me the time and space to write. Special thanks are due to Paul Harris for his quietly persistent prodding to keep me at it, and to

Anne Roussel who so kindly undertook to read the script and offered me many valuable suggestions. My thanks also go out to the many, many people from all over the world who have encouraged me by their own commitment to meditation for themselves and their children. And lastly, I wish to thank those who have shared with me their observations of specific children and have allowed me to use these in the book.

1

The Pedigree of Christian Mantra Meditation

This is a book about introducing children to Christian prayer; more specifically to that form of prayer which is called meditation, and more specifically still, to that form of meditation where a mantra is used throughout the time of prayer.

This may sound something like a conundrum but it is nothing of the sort; it is just a way of saying that I mean to treat of mantra meditation from within the context of Christian prayer. As a child belongs within a cherishing family and a flower shows to best advantage in its natural setting, so mantra meditation needs to be seen as one of the beautiful flowerings of the human heart's desire for its Lover–God.

Meditation is a fascinating word! It comes from the Latin *mederi* which means *to attend to*.[1] From this original derivation, or single source, have come two streams of meaning. One deals with the stimulation of thought and of the imagination, while the other turns away from both thought and imagination.

In the first stream, thought and imagination are called into play as a means of getting in touch with, *attending to*, the creative side of oneself. An interesting and valuable example of this understanding of meditation is seen in the work of Marguerite Smithwhite[2] among others. She aims to develop the deep inner potential of children by asking them to express themselves spontaneously on paper or in dance after a short period of attention during which she leads them, with their eyes closed, to imagine beautiful colours or a peaceful scene. The books of Deborah Rozman[3] also provide a rich source of information and practical ideas drawn from her years of experience. In the second stream, one is led to *attend to* the silence within oneself, just to BE with the One who is within and is the centre of all that is.

In the Christian tradition of prayer both these streams of meaning are found. Among the great teachers the first is seen as a preparation for, and a lead through to the second. In his *Ninth and Tenth Conferences*[4] the fourth-century Desert Father John Cassian emphasizes the importance of reflection on the Word through an assiduous reading of Scripture. He then advocates the constant repetition of a certain phrase, or formula as he calls it: 'O God, come to my assistance. O Lord, make haste to help me', to still the mind so that the word may go from the mind to the heart.

The theme of keeping the mind in the heart is central to the teaching of the Hesychast tradition, or the tradition of the Jesus Prayer as it is more familiarly known. In the fourth century, St Nicephorus, a monk of this tradition, had the quaint notion that, in the human anatomy, the lungs were wrapped around the heart. Thus breathing is a natural way to the heart he says, and continues:

And so, having collected your mind within you, lead it into the channel of breathing through which air reaches the heart and, together with the inhaled air, force your mind to descend into the heart and remain there . . . When you thus enter into the place of the heart, as I have shown you . . . keep always to this doing, and it will

8

teach you things which in no other way will you ever learn. Moreover, you should know that when your mind becomes firmly established in the heart, it must not remain there silent and idle, but it should constantly repeat the prayer: *Lord Jesus Christ, Son of God, have mercy on me*, and never cease.[5]

Here again, as in Cassian of the Desert Fathers, great importance is given to the continuous repetition of a phrase.

The anonymous fourteenth-century author of *The Cloud of Unknowing*[6] also teaches a constant repetition, but he favours the use of one word, and a short one at that, instead of a phrase as taught in both Desert and Hesychast traditions. He sees this little word as an instrument of love to knock on the cloud of unknowing which holds the presence of God. In Chapter 6 we read:

Strike that thick cloud of unknowing with the sharp dart of longing love, and on no account whatever think of giving up.

And Chapter 12 begins:

So if you are to stand and not fall, never give up your firm intention: beat away at the cloud of unknowing between you and God with that sharp dart of longing love.

He, too, subordinates the mind to the heart. Chapter 6 contains the following gem:

Though . . . we can know fully about other matters – yet of God himself can no man think. Therefore I will leave on one side everything I can think, and choose for my love that thing which I cannot think! By love he can be caught and held, but by thinking never.

In his *Spiritual Exercises*,[7] St Ignatius of Loyola, writing in the sixteenth century, uses both the words meditation and contemplation when referring to reflection upon the meaning of the Word of God in one's life. In this kind of meditation/contemplation Ignatius asks those who pray to enter imaginatively into a Gospel scene in order to be open to the experience of Christ in their own lives. Whatever the opening into the prayer, however, he always expects those who pray to rest and savour that which has special meaning for them. Stillness, depth and interior knowledge are the purpose of these methods of meditation and contemplation.

After the main body of the *Spiritual Exercises* Ignatius speaks of three Methods of Prayer helpful in ongoing daily life: Method Two is about the repetition of a phrase, for example by repeating one or other of the phrases of the Our Father, and Method Three is about repetition of a few words in the rhythm of breathing. These methods certainly find an echo in the kind of meditation which emphasizes simple repetition leading to depth and stillness. But Ignatius, it has to be said, does not lay stress on the constant repetition of a prayer word or phrase in the way that Cassian, the Hesychasts and the author of *The Cloud of Unknowing* do.

John Main, in his teaching, relates explicitly to this earlier tradition of the continuous repetition of a prayer word. As a pupil at a Jesuit school[8] his early training in prayer was Ignatian based according to the way it was then taught. A passage from the Gospels was given and one was invited to ponder over it with the help of two or three points from a book, ending with a prayer relevant to the subject.

10

As John matured into manhood, so his desire for a deepening prayer life led him to search for a form of prayer which would be real to him personally in his adult life. It was when he joined the Colonial Administrative Service and was posted to Malaya at the age of 29 that his hour struck.[9] He met a most remarkable man in the person of Swami Satyananda. Some twenty years later John Main wrote in *The Gethsemane Talks*:[10]

> I was deeply impressed by his peacefulness and calm wisdom . . . . He asked me if I meditated. I told him I tried to and, at his bidding, described briefly what we have come to know as the Ignatian method of meditation. For the swami, the aim of meditation was the coming to awareness of the Spirit of the universe who dwells in our hearts and he recited these verses from the Upanishads: 'He contains all things, all works and desires and all perfumes and tastes. And he enfolds the whole universe and, in silence, is loving to all. This is the Spirit that is in my heart. This is Brahman.'[11]

The swami saw the ultimate goal of prayer as becoming one with the Supreme Spirit:

> A serene and silent power is born in the soul of man in the depth of meditation . . . . Let us find the place of Peace – the island of spiritual fortifications in *the cave of the heart*. Let us be filled with the infinite even now.[12]

John Main had found his path of prayer. For eighteen months he went to meditate with the swami on his weekly free day, and with him he learnt to sit in stillness and silence while repeating a mantra. The swami told him that, as a Christian, he would do well to take a Christian mantra and he suggested the name Jesus.

It was not until many years later that he made the great discovery that this form of prayer, of keeping the mind in the heart through the repetition of a phrase or prayer word, had been in the Christian tradition from the earliest times. By then he was a Benedictine monk of fifteen years' standing and the remaining eight years of his life were devoted to reviving this ancient way of meditation, and presenting it in a form relevant to today.

While retaining the mantra tradition of Cassian, the Hesychasts and *The Cloud of Unknowing*, he brought to it the Eastern tradition of set periods of daily meditation which he had learnt from his teacher in Kuala Lumpur. Thus was born a way of Christian meditation, with the built-in discipline of twice daily periods, which could be practised by the busiest of people within their own life situation.

John Main encouraged people to meet with others in their locality on a weekly basis. It was soon found that the support received in thus meditating together was invaluable, and there are now hundreds of groups meeting regularly in many parts of the world.[13]

As a Benedictine he was committed to a daily pondering of the Scriptures and, as anyone who is familiar with his talks and writings will know, he placed the whole of his teaching within the context of the sacred texts, most particularly those of St John and St Paul.

Both the mulling over of the Scriptures and the twice daily periods of mantra meditation are important for anyone seriously following this way of prayer. There is always a danger, however, of remaining with the initial discursive form of meditation while rarely, if ever, progressing to the stillness, silence and simplicity of what the monks of old called 'pure prayer'. Yet, equally detrimental to the attainment of wholeness in prayer would be to neglect this pondering on the Scriptures altogether. There must always be a balance, with the study of Scripture acting as a handmaid to the silence of the prayer of the heart.

It is essential that meditation, in both these streams of meaning, be used in helping children into prayer, but it is with the second meaning, that of attending to the presence of God at the silent centre of one's being, that this book is dealing, and it is in this sense that the word meditation will be used throughout.

The derivation of the word contemplation can also help to enrich our understanding.[14] It comes from *templum*, a precinct, a sacred space or edifice, and *con-*, to view intensely or long. Originally, a temple was not necessarily a building, just a sacred space. Our innermost reality is indeed a sacred place. This place is symbolized in the fire of the burning bush when God says to Moses: 'Take off your shoes, for the place on which you stand is holy ground.'[15] God IS the sacred place at the centre of every human person.

Water is another scriptural symbol for this inner presence of God. Jesus tells the Samaritan woman at the well that the water he gives will become in him who drinks it 'a spring inside him welling up to eternal life'.[16] God IS the spring of living water at the core of our being. This is poetry-language and like all true poetry it has a thread of silence running through it leading us to the very centre of ourselves. In meditation we leave all to attend to this sacred space, this burning fire, this spring of living water in the silence within.

> The central silence is there
> where no creature may enter, nor any idea,
> and there the soul neither thinks nor acts

13

nor entertains any idea,
either of itself or of anything else.

Meister Eckhart[17]

Meister Eckhart frequently speaks of this central silence as 'the core of the soul'. It is interesting to come across this same word in a book about teaching Christian meditation to children:

Once invited into the silence and privacy of their own inner core, they [the children] simply come aglow. Theirs is a knowledge of contemplation that comes from within, a knowing that was present long before I ever met them. I cannot stress this enough. It does not take any technical knowledge to engage in contemplation. There are no course requirements, no necessary books to read. Everyone, especially every child, has an innate aptitude for contemplation.[18]

Admittedly the author is speaking of meditation using the imagination but it is equally true of imageless meditation. There is this innate aptitude for contemplation in each one of us. John Main is speaking of the same thing when he says in one of his talks:

The wonderful beauty of prayer is that the opening of our heart is as natural as the opening of a flower. To let a flower open and bloom it is only necessary to let it be; so if we simply are, if we become and remain still and silent, our heart cannot but be open, the Spirit cannot but pour through into our whole being. It is for this we have been created.[19]

Our approach therefore will be one of great respect for the person of each child as we nurture the God-given apti-

14

tude for contemplation. It is a matter of nurturing, never of imposing. The role of parents is essentially to nurture, and this must include a spiritual dimension arising from the spiritual commitment of parents and significant adults.

2

The Way to Teach or To Teach the Way

This chapter is arguably the most important in the whole book and we need to come back to it time and again. It deals with the foundations of our own spiritual life and so has an immediate bearing on our approach to the teaching of others, be they child or adult.

I have been asking myself why people might be interested in reading a book such as this. I decided that it could be for a good number of reasons, ranging from their wish to pass on to their children a form of prayer in which they have found strength, peace and truth, through a number of other persuasive reasons, to the extreme that was hissed at me a short time ago: 'Anything that will keep the little blighters quiet for a bit is worth a try!'

I then put the question to myself: 'Why do I think people will be interested in reading this book?' And again I found a good number of reasons ranging from the desire to do the best for one's children, to the reformation of society which would surely follow if prayer/meditation were to become widespread.

All valid reasons for reading a book on Christian meditation are necessarily interlinked because they are bound together by the faith that, with Jesus, we have 'our way to come to the Father'[1] as St Paul puts it. In our meditation we open ourselves in faith to the prayer, the life, the

16

consciousness of Jesus. It is only in the dark silence of our faith that we can enter into this mystery.

Concepts and words can only grope towards expressing the inexpressible and so it is useful constantly to remind ourselves that theological definitions and scriptural quotations, important as they are, can take us only so far, that they hide more than they reveal. What they hide are untold depths of mystery which cannot be spoken in human language or confined to human concepts.

As a human being, Jesus was limited by the common human inability to express the inexpressible in language and concept. He bypassed this problem by simply saying such things as: 'Come and see' and 'Follow me'.[2] Jesus never separated his teaching from himself. When he said: 'I am the Way, the Truth, the Life'[3] he made no effort to define Truth or Life or to reduce them to human concepts; all he told his disciples was that Truth and Life are found in him, that he himself is the Way of Truth and Life. It is only in this context that that other saying of Jesus': 'To have seen me is to have seen the Father'[4] can be approached.

From the time of the Resurrection his disciples appear to have called themselves both followers of Jesus and followers of the Way. It is evident from this that they realized that Jesus and his teaching were not to be separated. This is fundamental to the teaching of Paul in particular.

Take time to mull over in your mind and heart the following text from Paul's First Letter to the Corinthians and you will understand what I mean.

It was I who begot you in Christ Jesus by preaching the good news. That is why I beg you to copy me, and why I have sent you Timothy, my dear and faithful son in the Lord. He will remind you of the Way that I live in Christ, as I teach it everywhere in all the churches.[5]

17

People sometimes point a finger at Paul for begging us to copy him. Read in context, one can see that he can no longer think of himself apart from Christ. He is wedded to Christ and his disciples are born of Christ. Timothy, his dear disciple, is born of Christ and so are you and I as we live the Way in Christ. Listen to Paul again writing to the Colossians: 'God's message, in all its richness, must *live* in your hearts.'[6] The message is alive with Christ. Paul could never have conceived of it as a free-standing body of knowledge separate from Christ.

Paul was able to say 'Copy me' while remaining just as aware of his weaknesses as each of us is. Yet he does not, like us, look forward to the time when he will be perfect, having overcome all his faults. On the contrary, he views them in a very positive sense because it is patently clear to him that all the good he does is due to the power of Christ working in him.

I am most happy, then, to be proud of my weaknesses, in order to feel the protection of Christ's power over me. I am content with weaknesses, insults, hardships, persecutions and difficulties for Christ's sake. For when I am weak, then I am strong.[7]

Just as Paul centres his whole teaching on Christ, so do we. Like Paul we will accept our weaknesses happily and go ahead with confidence in our teaching. We will then have no difficulty in recognizing the power of Christ working, through us, in those we teach. We may even reach the point of humility when, with Paul, we will be able to exclaim: 'I beg of you to copy me.'

Classrooms are, by and large, places where bodies of knowledge are transmitted from a teacher to the taught. Danger signals start jangling in my head, therefore, when the classroom becomes the main platform for passing on the Way of Christ. For a teacher who is fully committed to Christ, the classroom could be a wonderful forum, but it is easy to see how the Way could become a free-standing body of knowledge on a par with other subjects on the curriculum, and divorced from the teacher's personal commitment to it.

It goes without saying that children, and particularly young children, are very susceptible to adult influence, and this lays upon us a grave responsibility. It calls for great respect, courtesy and gentleness on our part, within an ambience of loving affection. *It is all too easy to use overkill in order to control*. Overkill speaks in imperatives: 'Sit still' 'Be quiet' 'Come here'. Or threats: 'If you do that again I'll . . .'. Or condemnations: 'You naughty boy', 'You horrid girl'. This is not Jesus-speak, it is our own ego-speak. 'You should never help a baby walk because it falls down and cuts its knee and you always get a smack', so said Cormac, aged six.[8]

Nor is it advisable to go to the opposite extreme by covering children with a syruppy dose of 'Ooohs' and 'Aaahs' and 'What a clever girl you are!' and 'What a good boy!' by way of enhancing their self-esteem. In doing this we are unintentionally but emphatically shifting the motivation for learning and the satisfaction derived from it to external rewards and expectations of love and acceptance. Once, when visiting a class of six-year-olds, a boy asked me to listen to a story he had just written. While he was reading, I noticed he had drawn a number of tiny pictures throughout the text which did not seem to have anything to do with it. There was a little house, a man, a ball, a flower and more, all brightly coloured. So, when he had finished reading, I asked him about them. He sidled up close to me and said: 'When we make a mistake we don't cross it out; we make it look pretty.' Here, I felt, was a teacher after my own heart!

There can be no room for artificiality of any kind in our relationships with children, even if the intention is to help them think well of themselves. From birth, a child seeks to touch, taste, learn about and be one with everything. Joy comes from discovering the truths about how things are and how they work together. That is motivation and satisfaction enough. Madame Montessori was aware of this many years ago.

When we are aware of such weaknesses in ourselves, how can we be happy about them as Paul confesses he is? We need our weaknesses, he says, in order to feel the protection of Christ's power over us. Our very weakness gives us an acute awareness of our dependence on Christ, such as we would not have without this experience. And so we come full circle back to our meditation, when, twice daily, we put everything aside to withdraw into the power of Christ in the sanctuary of our inmost being and say our mantra in the darkness of our faith within the presence of Christ.

Let us now look at how we enter into this way of prayer. Find as quiet a place as you can, sit down with a straight back, close your eyes lightly and begin to say your prayer word or mantra. The mantra we recommend is *Maranatha*. Say it inwardly in four equal syllables: *Ma-ra-na-tha*. Do this for twenty minutes twice a day, coming back gently to it every time you get distracted, which will be often! But why such an odd word as '*Maranatha*'? John Main had good reason for suggesting this as a very suitable mantra, but he did not rule out the use of other mantras, the word *Abba* for example, which Jesus used in his own prayer. *Maranatha* is an Aramaic word meaning both *The Lord is coming* and *Lord, Come*. It is found in the very earliest Christian writings, calling upon the Lord Jesus to come in glory.

Paul ends his First Letter to the Corinthians, written in AD 57, with it:

20

Maranatha
The grace of the Lord Jesus be with you.
My love is with you all in Christ Jesus.[9]

It is interesting to find Paul leaving *Maranatha* in the original Aramaic while writing to these citizens of Corinth in their own Greek language. It has been suggested that this is because the word was already in current use among Christians as an expression of their longing for the veiled presence of Christ to be transformed into the revealed presence in the fullness of time.

Maranatha, this time translated into Greek, comes in the final summing up of the whole Bible in the Epilogue to the Book of Revelation.

The Spirit and the Bride say, 'Come' [*Maranatha*].
Let everyone who listens answer, 'Come'.
Then let all who are thirsty come:
all who want it may have the water of life
and have it free. . . .
The one who guarantees these revelations repeats
his promise: I shall indeed be with you soon.
Amen. COME, LORD JESUS.
May the grace of the Lord Jesus be with you all.
Amen.[10]

A passage in the *Didache*, a document which contains eucharistic prayers used in early Christian celebrations, also uses this prayer word, and again it expresses the Christian longing for the final coming of Christ in glory.

Hosannah to the God of David!
If anyone is holy, let him come;
if he is not, let him do penance.

21

Maranatha!
Amen.[11]

Now, twenty centuries later, we insert ourselves into this strong flowing river of longing for the final coming of the Lord Jesus who is already present in our hearts in faith, just as he was in the hearts of those early Christians as they, too, repeated the prayer word *Maranatha*.

This word sounding within you keeps away all thoughts, not only those about the hundred and one trivial things that generally fill our minds but also really good thoughts too, even thoughts about God, Mary and the saints. The whole of Chapter 7 of *The Cloud of Unknowing* is concerned with the topic of these good thoughts and the author insists that they be consigned to a cloud of forgetting during the time of what he calls 'the work'.

> . . . the practised hand must leave them [these thoughts], and put them away deep down in the cloud of forgetting if he is ever to penetrate the cloud of unknowing between him and God.[12]

In meditation we turn ourselves quietly and firmly away from all thought. This is what we have to lead our children to do, and we can only do it if we are practising it ourselves.

Did I hear you say that twenty minutes twice a day is impossible in your situation? Hundreds of people have said that before you and have lived to eat their words. If you really want to do it, there will be time. What about that bit of chatting that didn't lead anywhere? That TV programme that you didn't really mean to watch but just got hooked on once it had started? That bit of work that could have waited till tomorrow? It is all a matter of disciplining oneself! The surprising thing is that many people find they have more time for other things when they have disciplined themselves to this twice daily meditation. Try it!

Now what about those seemingly endless distractions? Does it mean that you are not suited to this kind of prayer? Nothing of the sort. They are just another form of that weakness that Paul was talking about. If you follow his advice once more you will take a positive view of them as you gently turn back to your mantra and, through it, to the life and the prayer of Christ within. Fifty-two distractions can mean 52 deliberate turnings back to the presence of God in the silence of your heart, and what more selfless prayer can there be than this? A distractionless period of meditation might be very comforting for you but it would not necessarily be a better meditation. The only valid assessment of meditation is a change in the quality of one's life over a period of time, and this is often noticed by those around us rather than by us ourselves. It will certainly be noticed by the children in our care.

I would say, however, that some distractions might need to be looked at more closely outside the time of meditation. It happens that anger, anxiety, grief and other material comes up from the unconscious when one begins to meditate. This is to be expected because, having been suppressed, now in the silence they have been freed to come into the conscious mind and affect our emotions. This is part of a healing process and, though painful, points the way to an inner freedom. It is a movement from pain to freedom, from death to resurrection.

It is important that these particular and persistent distractions be properly handled. Seek advice from a wise and sympathetic person – within the ranks of meditators such people are to be found. However, should these distractions cause distress, it would be sensible to talk with a trained counsellor. Meditation does not do away with the need for such support, it is not a means of covering over cracks but of bringing us to recognize our poverty, and part of our poverty is to do with acknowledging our need of others.

3

The First Years

A child's religious education begins, for better or worse, the day that the mother knows she is pregnant. The way in which she receives the news will influence the future of the embryo; and prior to that, both in time and importance, is the climate of relationship prevailing between father and mother; and behind that again is the ambience of the home.

Meditation during pregnancy is beneficial to both mother and child. For the mother it has a steadying influence, keeping mind and heart centred in the present, in the depths of her own being. Her unborn child is part of herself and participates in the calming effect of her meditation. At a deeper level, as the mother quietly focuses her whole person lovingly on God, she is preparing the way for a selfless, loving relationship between herself and her child. Anne, who came to practise meditation for the first time during her pregnancy told me how much it had helped her to develop a prayer relationship with the child she was carrying. After the birth she found it difficult to meditate unless he was on her lap, 'because' she said 'I have never meditated without James'.

Here is an extract from the letter of a first time mother full of simple joy and wonderment at the mystery of birth.

Our new baby has been born, and born safely. It is a little

boy with brown hair and olivy skin. It is all hard to believe. I meditated with him today, and now that all the midwives and doctors have stopped coming, I hope to settle back into our meditation times. I am sure meditation helped him through pregnancy. It is all so hard to believe; it really is a miracle how God creates humanity. I feel he really is a gift from God because nothing man-made could create a child – suffer the little children to come unto me.

Yet another mother writes:

One of my special memories is of giving Martin his feed in the early hours of the morning when the whole world seemed to be asleep. I used to enjoy being with God and my baby, and I prayed deeply at this time. I am sure it affected Martin.

And another:

Stroking a very small baby's head during meditation I found communicates stillness and peace and deepens relationships.

A mother, looking lovingly at her baby, is in effect saying: 'Surprise me! Give me a first smile! Recognize me!' This attitude of waiting to be surprised by a child is the surest way of encouraging the development of his or her potential.

The newborn baby clings to its mother for its very existence; it loves her for the food, warmth and comfort without which it cannot survive. One could say that its love is initially predominantly selfish. It is from this infant love that the human person sets out on the path towards a love that is completely selfless.

This journey from selfish to unselfish love is mirrored in Shakespeare's Seven Ages of Man, from '. . . the infant mewling and puking in the nurse's arms' to the finality of 'sans teeth, sans eyes, sans taste, sans everything'. But there is one great difference. In the spiritual lifespan this situation of being without everything is the ultimate attainment of selflessness – a selflessness built up gradually through the living out of the other stages of life. The whining schoolboy with his satchel and shining morning face, the sighing lover writing a woeful ballad to his mistress' eyebrow, the soldier full of strange oaths, the justice with beard of formal cut and the big manly voice turning again towards childish treble, signalling the time of diminishment, are all imaged in our spiritual journey towards that selfless love which is without power, without fame, without future, without everything save the pure love of God himself in our hearts.

In these first years practically all a child's learning comes through the senses, hence the importance of positive and happy experiences in the home. Touch, of course, is the most elemental of the senses and is intimately connected with the trauma of birth and the comfort of the first feed. Touch can be a potent, wordless way of showing affection, and children, in these home years before school age is reached, have a great need of being held, cuddled, carried. Such physical contact with an adult who is meditating regularly is a real bonus because it brings a spiritual dimension to the intimacy between mother and child at a deep level, and completes the cycle of union.

Next in time comes the physical experiencing by the child of its immediate world; the world of its own toes and fingers, hands, face and body, and the world of things: gentle things like the bath water and an animal's fur, hard things, smooth and rough things, sharp things, sticky things and slippery things. All these experiences relating to the sense of touch provide a medium for the development of wonder, and wonder is prayer in embryo.

At the same time, of course, the child is beginning to come to terms with the world through the other senses and these experiences equally lead through into wonder. You have only to see a tiny baby lying on its back, watching the world go by and allowing all the messages that are being registered by the eyes and ears and tongue and touch to sink in, to know that wonderment is inborn.

In the first months and years children are very sensitive to order and routine. It stands to reason when you remember that this is essentially the First Time Period of life. Everything is being seen, felt, touched, smelled, heard for the first time, and out of this jumble of experiences the baby has to make sense. If the jumble is compounded by a total lack of order and routine, the child lives through this immensely important stage of life without gaining a solid basis for its future development. It remains unsure as to who it is and where it belongs.

This chapter is concerned mainly with the mewling and puking stage of life when order and routine, both forms of repetition, the one of place, the other of time, are of prime importance. The saying: 'A place for everything and everything in its place' is just what these little ones need: the mug is taken from and goes back to the same place, and everything else has its own place. This gives security in a puzzling world.

Routine is repetition applied to time. There are bathing times, playing-with-Mummy times, times for being awake and playing with one's toes, going out times, feeding times and sleeping times. It is during these sleeping times that Mummy could make her own routine of meditating beside the cot, maybe crooning the word Jesus as a lullaby till the child is asleep. The name of Jesus will be suggested as a child's first mantra in a later chapter. Times of regular meditation in the house are as important for your child as they are for you, so remember this when you may be tempted to skip them.

The father of several children writes:

Light mornings bring another factor into meditation. Our youngest, Miriam, tends to appear before due time and whiles away the time by using Dad's crossed legs as a park bench. I noticed, though, that she and Claire the other morning were silent for ten minutes, so perhaps something rubs off!

The crawling and then the toddling age present the greatest challenge to the parents' meditation routine. Once steady on its feet, a child gradually acquires the freedom of the house and is in a position to explore and to gain first hand experience of anything and everything. An exciting, if dangerous, period both for the child and for the adults. The constant vigilance required to ensure that television knobs are not tampered with, that the cat is not rubbed up the wrong way and that fingers are not pinched in the door, can be quite a test when it comes to meditation times. A previously established routine will pay dividends both in strengthening a faltering resolve on the part of the adult and in leading the child to accept meditation as much a part of the daily round as the washing of teeth and the brushing of hair. For a time it may continue to be possible to meditate while the child is asleep in the afternoon, but the day will come when he/she is fully awake during the time of meditation.

In a wordless way it will be known that Mum, or preferably both parents, have their time of quiet with God morning and evening. These are *God times* and there is quiet in the house. No explanations are necessary, no verbal teaching given. This is part of the culture into which the child has been born and it is assimilated in the same way as the parents' language and way of life.

The child understands that he/she will be welcome at meditation, either cuddled for a time on a parent's lap or close beside. The rest of the time could be spent sitting on the floor with some quiet toys. A special box with such things as picture books, crayons and paper, a doll for dressing and undressing, and building blocks might be kept in the room specifically for use during meditation times.

This fluid introduction to meditation will remain available throughout childhood; some will join in for longer periods as they grow older, others will opt out. Both options must be seen as acceptable so that the more tractable will not be tempted to continue to meditate so as to curry favour with the adults while the others acquire a guilt complex.

We are brought to wonder when we are faced with something which is beyond our capacity to comprehend, something which is a mystery and which leaves us speechless. We are, in fact, whether we know it or not, brought up short before the mystery whom we call God. Our contribution as adults is one of enabling the child or children in our care to be free and fearless, so that unexpectedly, rapturously, in some unforeseen moment of contact, they may be caught up in this mystery of God.

Here are some adults speaking of childhood experiences which they could not have formulated at the time even if they had had the language.[1] The experience was, and always is, instantaneous. Words are heavy and inadequate but they are the only way we have of trying to communicate the incommunicable.

My first remembered experience of the numinous occurred when I was barely three. I recall walking down a little cul-de-sac lane behind our house in Shropshire. The sun was shining, and as I walked along the dusty lane, I became acutely aware of the things around me. I noticed a group of dandelions on my left at the base of the stone wall. Most of them were in full bloom, their golden heads irradiated by the sun, and suddenly I was overcome by an extraordinary feeling of wonder and joy. It was as if I was part of the flowers and stones and dusty earth. I could feel the dandelions pulsating in the sunlight, and experienced a timeless unity with all life. It is quite impossible to express this in words, or to recall its intensity. All I know now is that I knew something profound and eternal then.

I owe my early religious ideas and feelings to the influence of my family . . . I remember particularly a great aunt known to be very devout, of extreme sweetness of disposition, and a colleague of my father's who gave me the serious attention accorded to adults. It was easy to talk about God to both these people. However, the special experiences I had in this period, unheralded moments of beatitude and felicity, not caused by any incident, were, it seems to me now, separate from these influences, although the latter may have provided in part my receptivity to the outside. They invaded me unawares.

Until I was seven, religion was purely external, expressed perhaps by the nursery jingle 'one two three four five six seven, all good children go to heaven', 'There is a green hill' etc. Then in Standard II of a Wesleyan School I had an extraordinarily vivid insight which is absolutely beyond description but which has remained with me ever since as an abiding spiritual experience. The teacher was explaining that in addition to common nouns and proper nouns there were also abstract nouns which mostly ended in -ness, such as goodness, badness; also a number of short but very important words such as love, hate, etc. It was at this point that I seemed to grow up mentally. The fact that it was completely ineffable does not puzzle me in the least since it appears to have been a common experience of contemplatives to be unable to find words to describe what they have inwardly experienced.

And this one from an Irish person with a strong religious background:

My mother took me into a church where there was exposition of the Blessed Sacrament. I was three and a half or four years of age. Taking Blessed Sacrament beads out of her bag she told me to say:

O Sacrament most holy
O Sacrament divine.
All praise and all thanksgiving
Be every moment thine.

I began to say that little verse not knowing or realizing what it meant and was completely wrapped in God's love. As I did not understand what happened I did not tell my mother or anyone. When I was nine or ten I went into my parents' room and saw the beads, broken, lying on my mother's dressing table. Recalling what I had experienced as a little girl I began to recite the little verse hoping to bring back the gift, but I did not succeed. Years later, I read in St Theresa of Avila that these gifts cannot be induced.

In no way is it being suggested that we should be foolish enough to try to induce such intuitions of God, and particularly not during the time of meditation. Our contribution, as was said earlier, is one of enabling children to be open and fearless, with psychological space to be themselves, unselfconscious and free from the pressures which often cause them to live in a state of acute anxiety.

You will notice that not one of these children was looking for or expecting an experience of God, and that only one such experience happened within a religious context. They were just being themselves in their normal situation. What it tells us is that God is active in each of our lives, always breaking through in his own way and time, and that this happens quite frequently in childhood.

So let us tread like angels. Children have something precious in their innocence and directness which is lost when we become caught up in the coils of adult living, as instanced by this childhood memory:

> I remember sitting in my mother's lap at the age of five, while she affectionately explained that the idea of God was a very nice and poetic way of explaining things, but just like a fairy tale. I felt embarrassed at what seemed abysmal blindness and ignorance and felt sorry for her.[2]

4

The Home

Most homes are reasonably orderly and, as suggested in the last chapter, this is immensely important for the small child during the First Time Period of life. This orderliness, along with the security of being loved and wanted, will give the child a firm foundation from which to set out on the journey into life.

St Augustine has a saying about making a stepping-stone of oneself so that 'one may rise thence and be borne up to God'.[1] A foundation is one thing, but a stepping-stone is more: a foundation which also helps one on one's way, so it expresses well the function of a home with respect to the child or children within it.

The home as a stepping-stone is quite a thought. During childhood it seems so permanent; the child cannot envisage life as other than at home, but when we look back as adults, we have no trouble in realizing that our childhood was the base, for better or worse, from which we stepped out into adult life. All parents know that the time will come when they will be called upon to assist in the difficult transition from childhood to adulthood, and much of the success of this transition will depend upon the relationship built up in the earliest years.

Parents' attitudes are assimilated at a particularly profound level during the first two and a half crucial years of a child's life. These attitudes are absorbed below the

34

threshold of consciousness and are imprinted more vividly in the child than the lifetime of spoken teaching, addressed to the conscious level, which will follow. But still more profound is the influence of one's personal attitudes which a child will assimilate through his/her whole being.

This is well put by the Nigerian writer Ben Okri in his novel *The Famished Road*.[2] One night the compound catches fire and in the ensuing riot the child Azaro is separated from his mother and gets lost. After many terrifying adventures she finds him and takes him to the makeshift accommodation where she and her husband are now living. The child says: 'But in that room, in our new house, I was happy because I could smell the warm presences and the tender energies of my parents everywhere.' Home is where parents are, whether in a shack or a mansion, and is created by their presence and tender energies. Where, instead, the energies are of anger and rancour, these will enter into the child's innermost being instead.

The home itself should be a place of pleasing experiences for each of the senses. Plants and flowers about the house, Mum's perfume of an evening, quiet background music if you are that kind of family, and pictures that you yourself love, not to mention the occasional delicious aroma arising from the kitchen. Appetizing meals are also very important. All these things, and many others, enter into the deepest memory of a child never to be eradicated.

Smell is the most evocative of the senses: home smells such as ironing, furniture polish, carpets, cushions and the sheet cupboard, belong for life, but these need to be supplemented by outdoor smells, sights and sounds to enrich the sense vocabulary. The town child can and does relate positively to the hustle and bustle of traffic, shopping precincts and screaming police cars as instanced by a girl of eleven living in a one-time London slum who wrote a poem which she entitled 'Grime'. She ended each verse with the refrain 'Oh the dear dirt of London'. This was her home situation and she loved it. Perhaps she was also alert to the beauty of a street lamp reflected in a puddle and the moon rising over a row of chimney pots. The poet will out.

However, most town children now have access to parks, ponds and green areas to enlarge the scope of their appreciation. Even so, they may need some stimulation from an adult as the following extract from a letter shows. This is from a teacher in a city school:

I was inspired to take my lunch hour Poetry Workshop group to a nearby park to enjoy the flowers and trees. I was curious to know how many of them could distinguish the different kinds of trees. I found them very ignorant! So I began to take a leaf as a sample for each common tree. This started to extend to flowers. They didn't seem much interested at first, but then suddenly they warmed up and started looking around them with the greatest enthusiasm, and I had difficulty restraining them from diving into front gardens to pick flowers to add to my bunch. These were 11–13 year olds. They were so happy it was really wonderful. We decided to take our lunch and go for the whole lunch break next week.

It would be ideal, though not always possible I know, to have a small area in the house, perhaps in a corner of a room, set aside as a prayer space. This could take the form of a little table or shelf which is always kept sacred. The table could be furnished with a candle, a small statue or holy picture and fresh flowers in season. It should be a homely place where children and adults place things which have meaning for them at the moment, a reminder of an absent friend, a feather or lovely stone found during a walk, a piece of moss or a spray of autumn leaves. It would be in this area that meditation would take place.

If a young child shows signs of wanting to be present for a few minutes of the meditation, a little prayer mat might be introduced. It would be special to meditation and would underline the idea of sacred space and silence. Removing shoes before meditation also serves the same purpose.

Thought needs to be given to children's bedrooms. A young child spends quite a large proportion of its time in its bedroom, so let the furnishings be simple, clean and light when possible, with one or two interesting pictures. A plain cross or crucifix might occupy a place of honour either in the bedroom or on a landing. A young Catholic mother told me that, as a means of inculcating respect in a wordless way, she used to pause and make a bow in front of the crucifix on the landing when carrying her little child to and from the bedroom. One word of caution though: realistic crucifixes, most especially painted ones with blood flowing from the wounds, must be banned from any house where there are young children. They have caused nightmares and terror to many children. I remember being told that a boy of six whom I knew had to be carried kicking and screaming into his bedroom at night till it was discovered that he was scared of the painted crucifix on the wall opposite his bed!

Many traditional Catholic families like to have statues, holy pictures and holy water about the home as well as a candle to be lit at special times. Simple rituals celebrating family events can make a deep impression on a child. Blessing the house with holy water, sprinkling a child's bedroom while saying a short prayer of blessing, making the sign of the cross on the forehead in a little ritual before sleep, lighting a candle in a storm as a reminder of the presence of Jesus, and the lighting of the child's baptismal candle on each birthday, are all well-tried Christian customs which are full of spiritual meaning.

It is in these simple ways that the foundations of prayer are laid. They could, in fact, be called stepping-stones to God because they develop that sense of wonder at the core of the personality on which we are 'borne up to God' as St Augustine says. Jacques Cousteau, the great underwater explorer, puts it another way, perhaps one we can relate to more easily.

Like most fathers, by clear star-studded skies I used to take my two little boys in my arms for a glimpse at infinity. The splendour of the unreachable silenced these chatterboxes for a few moments. They raised their arms and closed their little fingers in a futile attempt to grasp one of the twinkling sparks that dot our dreams. They were obeying the command reported by Ovid: 'God elevated man's forehead and ordered him to contemplate the stars.'[3]

Here is another such example, this time of a father with his daughter. When the daughter was in her twenties she told me that she had been brought up on a small farm in western Ireland. One evening she accompanied her father on an evening walk around the perimeter of his property. As they turned into a certain field, there before them was a most wonderful sunset. Her father did not say anything but just sat down on the edge of the field, and she beside him. Together they watched the glory before them until it had faded. Then he got up and they went on home. Her father had said nothing at all but that young woman dates her appreciation of nature from that particular evening and incident.

Wonder is brought about by an experience of mystery; we look at a sunset or the fairyland of lights as our plane passes over a great city at night, and we experience a sense of awe which keeps us silent before something which cannot be encompassed by words. This experience of mystery gives birth to, or flows over into, a prayer of silent adoration as it brings us to the ultimate mystery whom we call God and whom Jesus called Father. Prayer was described by Evagrius in the fourth century as the raising of the mind and heart to God by the laying aside of thoughts. In wonder, both mind and heart are first engaged and then superseded as we enter into a profound silence before the mystery of God. This is just what meditation is all about.

5

The Fostering of Wonder

With the advent of the human race the universe was able, for the first time, to reflect upon itself. The 'Who am I?' question became possible. It is, in fact, the essential human question, and it is a question that leads directly into wonder.

Our ability to wonder brings us up short as it focuses us on things which are beyond our ability to comprehend and which, in the final analysis, always lead back to the same 'Who am I?' question. This question is posed by poets and scientists alike and we need to remember that there is a potential poet and scientist within each one of us wondering, probing, searching and delving further into the mystery of who we are.

Small children have all the time in the world to wonder about the 'Who am I?' question at their own level. They do it experientially, trying out what their hands, their feet and their bodies can do. Our simplest nursery rhymes celebrate this propensity. Finger and hand rhymes such as 'This little pig went to market' and 'Pat-a-cake, pat-a-cake baker's man' abound in many cultures and who has not seen children trying out how far they can run, how long they can hold their breath?

Alongside this interest in their own persons goes an investigation of their immediate environment. They experience water, earth, grass, sunlight, and a myriad of other things which are the stuff of the universe. Parents can do much to foster this learning in their children by finding the time to play with them and by giving them the opportunity and the confidence to explore their immediate universe, a universe of which they are part.

Two friends of mine were sitting on the sand at Whitley Bay while Katie, the two-and-a-half-year old daughter of one of them, occupied herself nearby. Having found a gull's feather she spent a long time looking at it, feeling it and turning it every way. She then rested it on the water and watched it being carried a little way away and then being brought back on a wave. She picked it up again and continued to play with it like this for the best part of half an hour. The two friends were forcibly struck by the sheer wonder which had taken possession of that child for so long, and they realized how much they, as adults, were missing out on. They had, however, provided this wonderful opportunity for Katie just TO BE, without interference, in communion with the universe.

Speaking to Catholic Italian teachers, Pope John Paul II stressed the importance of creating conditions for children to acquire a greater awareness of their faith. He mentioned the first attitude to develop in them as *attention*, and continued:

> This requires that you help your students not to suffocate but rather to nourish their innate amazement in the face of creation and to reflect on it in order to grasp its perfection. To educate to this attitude, it is indispensible that the child be led to a real and profound interior *silence* which is the first requisite for listening.[1]

Except in certain inner city areas trees, grass, water and wild wind can be found not too far away from most people's homes. The more ecologically privileged ones will be within reach of walks in woods, climbs up hills and experiences of streams, rivers or seashores. There is a certain capacity for learning which is unique to childhood and these experiences sink deeply into the very core of a child's being in a way that is no longer possible in later life. This is the precious time for laying the foundations for a lifetime of growing into the understanding that through us this breath-takingly beautiful universe is able to reflect upon itself, to appreciate the beauty of a sunset, the majesty of a mountain or the beguiling simplicity of a daisy. Using this ability to reflect, scientists are ceaselessly engaged in delving further and further into the wonders of the universe, and we find the same urge among the artists:

> When we speak of Nature it is wrong to forget that we are ourselves a part of Nature. We ought to view ourselves with the same curiosity and openness with which we study a tree, the sky or a thought, because we too are linked to the entire universe.
>
> Henri Matisse[2]

> The artist is a receptacle for emotions that come from all over the place; from the sky, from the earth, from a scrap of paper, from a passing shape, from a spider's web. Where things are concerned there are no class distinctions.
>
> Pablo Picasso[3]

> The habit of ignoring Nature is deeply implanted in our times. This attitude reminds me of people who never look you in the eye. I find them disturbing and always have to look away.
>
> Marc Chagall[4]

It is imperative that we relinquish the immature dualistic idea of a God up in the sky, directing the universe from a distance. To quote Thomas Berry: 'Good people are dangerous when they are operating out of assumptions about reality which do not in fact correspond to reality.'

We cannot say that God is one with the universe in the sense that he is synonymous with it. We may be nearer the truth if we say that God is one with the universe but the universe does not contain him. Here, once more, we are in the realm of mystery which can never be adequately expressed in words. Mystery begets wonder which, let me say again, leads us into that profound silence before the Source of Being whom we call God. Meditation is born of this wonder and leads us into that profound silence.

Tom, aged six, wrote this: 'Dear God, thank you for all your special power for spring. Love Tom', and it was accompanied by a drawing of three flowers with strong energy charges through them. What more beautiful prayer could one wish for, full of wonder at the mystery of nature springing into life after winter? Gerard Manley Hopkins expressed just such an insight when he wrote: 'The world is charged with the grandeur of God.'

Tom's granny told me: 'It was a spontaneous effort. While I was washing up, he said "I'm going to write a letter to God and throw it up into the sky." ' Someone, somewhere, most certainly with the best of intentions, had told him this fanciful tale about God living in the sky. How much better if he had been encouraged from the very beginning to respond to the wonders of nature by closing his eyes and spending a few moments *being with God within* while quietly repeating the words: 'Dear God'. When he had this moment of realization about the power of spring, he would then quite naturally have remained silent with God within, maybe repeating the mantra 'Dear God' for a moment or two. Far from having to be unlearnt later on, this would have been a genuine growth in relationship with God valid for life.

'That's no lion. That's my Mum!' was the exasperated retort I received from a six-year-old as he turned to face me from the easel, dripping paint brush held high. The painting in question was of a circular orange face with two brown blobs for eyes, two smaller blobs for nostrils, a long moon-shaped brown mouth and a profusion of darkish orange loops all round the face which, to me, was quite clearly a mane. Silly me! Mine was the typical adult reaction. We are so used to looking at a work of art and taking the most obvious and literal meaning from it. That child was not trying to express what his mother looked like – one only had to look at her to know that – but to portray her warmth and her comforting person. To that child orange must have seemed the most beautiful colour of all. It was an effort to express all that his mother meant to him, and along comes this stupid grown-up with an inane remark about it being lion!

Henri Matisse would never have made my mistake. Listen to what he says:

> The task of painting is no longer to portray historical events. We can read about those in books. We must expect more of painting. It can serve the artist to express his inner visions. You have to know how to preserve that freshness and innocence a child has when it approaches things. You have to remain a child your whole life long and yet be a man who draws his energy from the things of the world.[5]

Artists and poets are people who have been able to retain that inwardness and clarity of vision and who then express it in terms of their own culture and personality. Stanley Spencer says this:

> We all go down to Odney Weir for a bathe and a swim.

44

I feel fresh, awake and alive; this is the time for visitation . . . I swim in the pathway of the sunlight; I go home thinking of the beautiful wholeness of the day. During the morning I am visited and walk about in that visitation. In the afternoon I set out my work and begin the picture. I leave off at dusk feeling delighted with the spiritual work I have done.[6]

And again, when employed as a war artist and painting the men at work at Port Glasgow, he wrote:

. . . the concentrated activity of the men in the ship-yards inspired a kind of awe. I was as disinclined to disturb them as I would be to disturb a service in the church.[7]

Here, to support the contention that children are true artists, are two more examples to illustrate the point. Ann, aged six, wrote: 'My mother has witish yellow hare, pink-ish eyes and lots of teeth and is very butifull.'[8] Ann was only aware of what her mother meant to her and she summed it up in the words 'very butifull'. Hair, eyes and mouth all expressed the loving relationship between them.

I have a precious drawing by a Finnish boy aged three-and-a-half. Again, it is of his mother. Two eyes and some hair represent the head and, coming from this on either side, are two well-defined lines reaching to the bottom of the page. When his mother asked him what these were, he answered: 'Long, long arms so you can hold all the children in the world.' How we need to attend to the artist and the poet in our children!

Perhaps the most immediate lesson in all this is for our-selves, to sensitize us to that source of pure artistry within every child which is of an exquisite fragility like the sparkle in a dew drop or colours in a bubble. It is so very easy to destroy the dew drop or prick the bubble. We need to respect this fragile gift of interiority and to be prepared to repair the damage if, heavy-footed, we have mistaken the most beautiful Mum in the world for a lion!

We will learn so much if we discipline ourselves really to listen to children as Jesus surely did. We will then understand something of the awe which led him to exclaim in gratitude to the Father and thank him for showing to little children things which are hidden from the wise and learned.[9] We will become increasingly open to, and appreciative of the freshness of their insights.

Let us respect their need for times of silence and aloneness, and may we never talk down to them, however young; this betrays an uncomprehending arrogance on our part. Equally, let us never talk over their heads to other adults as though they did not exist or were just part of the furniture.

With the special sensitivity for learning which children have, they very soon pick up vibes that lead them to feel inadequate in the presence of the adults around them, and they can so easily feel themselves to be a disappointment to their parents when in reality there is much that is spiritual that parents can learn from them, including how to meditate in great simplicity.

This fostering of the artistic side of children relates to one meaning of the verb 'to educate'. *Educere* means 'to lead out', 'to draw forth' what is latent in the child. The other meaning of the verb is *educare* which basically means to impose the mores of whatever culture the child has been born into. This spans the whole area from learning how to brush one's teeth, to school and university learning and beyond. It includes, of course, one's initiation into the faith culture of the family. Up until the Middle Ages, the churches and cathedrals provided for this wholeness in religious education. There the stories of both Old and New

46

Testaments were painted and sculpted round the interior and were depicted in the stained glass. The mystery plays brought in yet another medium of learning, but perhaps music provided the most powerful stimulus of all. The wonderful plainsong melodies arose from, and led right back into the mystery of prayer.

Nor must the dance be forgotten. Religious dance goes back to earliest times, and the tradition of Jesus as Lord of the Dance is found in the Gnostic Acts of John where Jesus not only sings the hymn before going to his passion but bids the disciples form a ring holding one another's hands and, going about, answer 'Amen' to his prayer. The symbolic reference is to the total acceptance of, and abandonment to, the will of his Father. This tradition was still alive in the Middle Ages as St Bernard sings:

> Jesus the dancers' master is.
> A great skill at the dance is his.
> He turns to right, he turns to left.
> All must follow his teaching deft.[10]

Our own homes, our own schools must now be our cathedrals, our sacred places, where the arts can be brought to bear in providing our children with a wholeness of religious education. And within that wholeness, protected by it and, in a real sense, developed through it, lies the gift of prayer, the *pure prayer* of meditation.

The other great source of wonder is science and the natural world. Within the last few years scientists have been able to assert that the whole cosmos, with its thousands of galaxies, was present in essence in the original fireball. The primeval cloud was a great sheaf of possibilities and one of these was the sun. Some four-and-a-half billion years ago a giant red star exploded and in that moment the sun was born and began to organize itself. It might never have been born if the explosion had been different. With no sun there would have been no earth and hence no present moment. This gives us food, not so much for thought – precisely because it is utterly beyond our thought processes – as for a wonder which, once again, leads us into a profound silence at the Source of Being.

The Desert Father, John Cassian, sees this profound silence as the fruit of *purity of heart*. He says:

> No one is kept away from purity of heart by not being able to read, nor is rustic simplicity any obstacle to it, for it lies close at hand for all if only they will by constant repetition of this phrase keep the mind and heart attentive to God.[11]

Cassian recommended a phrase, the author of *The Cloud of Unknowing* a short word, preferably a word of one syllable, John Main the word *Ma-ra-na-tha*. One can take one's choice because the aim, to remain in profound silence with God, who is pure Being, is the same in each case and in meditation we celebrate this presence within.

The whole area of cosmology was largely ignored in our Christian catechesis until quite recently but this gap can no longer be tolerated. There is a crying need for teachers, professional or otherwise, to study cosmology so as to be able to mediate its principles to children of whatever age. Books that will speak to five-year-olds through to those for school leavers would find a ready market in all parts of the religious world.

Thomas Berry's *Dream of the Earth*,[12] Brian Swimme's *The Universe is a Green Dragon*[13] and his video series *A Canticle to the Cosmos*[14] along with Michael Dowd's *Earthspirit*[15] provide dynamic source material with which to start such a study. Mention might also be made of *At Home on Planet Earth*[16] which has many practical ideas for young people though, having been published before the latest break-through in cosmology, a revised edition would be wel-come. *The Home Planet,*[17] composed exclusively of what astronauts have written about their experiences, is one unbroken tissue of material for wonder.

Let us explore the subject a little more so as to help us experience that great 'Oh!' of awe and wonder which is there within us waiting to be brought to life.

The Earth is a special planet. It has come about because it is exactly the right size and the right distance from the sun to sustain life. It may help us to glimpse an understanding of this if we take a look at Mars and Jupiter, our neigh-bouring planets. The pressures of gravity and electromag-netism on Mars, which is smaller than Earth, were of such an order that the crust got thicker and thicker until it became so solid that the planet's development was choked off. Jupiter, on the other hand, is much larger than Earth. There these same pressures were of an order that the planet has remained gaseous; there is no solid land and no life.

Planet Earth, however, is exactly the right size for these two pressures to be balanced and, precisely because of this, Earth can develop and produce life. It is semi-liquid, not solid throughout. Rocks are formed and then break down; atmosphere and oceans are formed and life comes forth.

> If the earth had been smaller
> life would have been choked off.
> If the earth had been larger
> life would never have happened.[18]

The story of the Three Bears is of mythic proportions! The Earth is neither too small like Mars nor too large like Jupiter, but is just right for expansion and life, and every child of Earth is a growing point for the energy of the universe to develop in new and ever surprising ways. This is 'Who I am!'

6

The Risen Christ

It is our relationship with the risen Christ which identifies us as true Christians. Our one way of building up this relationship in our children is through the stories of Jesus when he was on earth in Palestine. But always we need to bring them forward from then to that same Jesus who is with us now, risen and glorified. And before we can do this, we ourselves must pause and think about who this risen Jesus is.

For the last two thousand years so many images of Jesus have been projected, all reflecting the culture and history of their time and place, that we might well be confused. Jesus was presented in the catacombs as a beardless, youthful shepherd; in the Byzantine era, as a bearded Emperor and Ruler of the world; in Chartres Cathedral as the *Beau Dieu*; on the Romanesque portals and apses as the King and Judge of the world enthroned on the Cross; and in Raphael's 'Disputa' as a handsome Christ untouched by suffering. Michaelangelo portrayed him as a very human, suffering Christ, while the Catholic late baroque pictures of the Sacred Heart present us with a distinctly sentimental Jesus. Then there is the meek and mild Jesus of the Pre-Raphaelite painting of Christ knocking at the door of our heart; whilst a very different dimension is pointed to by artists such as Rouault along with many other twentieth century artists. And what about the field of music? Is Jesus the 'Joy of Man's Desiring' or the judge figure of the much earlier 'Dies Irae'?

While not denying the validity, in varying degrees, of these images, it must be abundantly clear that the reality of the human person called Jesus cannot be known from Christian piety or literature or art in any objective way. We must go directly to the New Testament and the Church's teaching which is drawn from it, the teaching that Jesus Christ is truly man and truly God.

The Gospels present us with a picture of Jesus as a human being of great stature. While there have been heresies in the past which denied that Jesus was truly human, we need not spend time on discussing them here. We can accept, from the evidence of the Gospels, that Jesus was, and is, truly a man. But in what sense are we to believe that Jesus Christ is truly God?

To say that Jesus Christ is truly God means that the true man Jesus of Nazareth is the real revelation of the one true God, the One beyond name and form. That God is beyond name and form lies deep within the Jewish faith and Scriptures. The name of God is never to be pronounced for this very reason, that he is beyond all names, and no image of God is to be tolerated because God is beyond all forms. In Christian teaching, Jesus gives both name and form to God. He is the full expression or revelation of the Father.

How does he communicate this revelation of the Father to us? Before Jesus died and was resurrected, people knew him *in the flesh* to use St Paul's term. They saw him face to face and judged him to be either a holy man, a great prophet, or a threat to their way of life and a man to be got rid of. This was the historical Jesus with whom they had physical contact and about whose earthly life we read in the Gospels.

Since his resurrection he can no longer be seen and known *in the flesh*, that is, as he used to be when he walked the roads and hills of Palestine during the 33 years or so of his earthly life. St Paul puts it this way:

> Even if we did once know Christ *in the flesh*, that is not how we know him now.[1]

During his earthly life he was known *in the flesh*; since his death and resurrection he is known *in the Spirit*. It is *in the Spirit* that the risen Christ communicates himself to us as the revelation of the Father. This is what is meant when we say that God himself is manifested, shown, revealed, *through* Jesus Christ, *in the Spirit*. The ancient Roman collects (prayers) of the liturgy all end with a formula of praise to the Father, *through* the Son, *in* the Holy Spirit. This prayer-ending, known as a doxology, has been used in the Church ever since. It expresses the central teaching of the Church about who Jesus is.[2]

Now let us return to our children at home. We are not going to repeat to them this exposition of the Church's teaching. But it is of supreme importance that we speak out of this understanding of Jesus as he was in his earthly life, and of the risen, glorified Jesus as he is now: the Jesus *in the flesh* and the Jesus *in the Spirit*. 'Even if we did once know Christ in the flesh, that is not how we know him now.'

During his life on earth Jesus' relationships were subject to the limitations which are inherent in all relationships between human beings in this life. We relate to others through sight, touch, speech and hearing, and also through intuition and telepathy. In every case it is our earthly being which is the medium of communication. We are in the flesh and communicate through the flesh, to use St Paul's phrase once more. And so it was with Jesus.

In order to begin to know Jesus, who is with us *in the Spirit* now, we will introduce him to our children as he was when he walked the paths of this planet. Through the stories of his life, the way he reacted to people, his friends and disciples, the sick, the poor and outcasts of society and their oppressors, they will begin to build up a picture of Jesus. But this Jesus, we tell them, who lived and died so long ago, is still with us now. He told his friends: 'Know that I am with you always; yes, to the end of time.'[3] This is sufficient, without explanation, for children who are still below what has become known as the age of reason.

Until about the age of three, our way of introducing Jesus will be, like all our teaching at that age, mainly implicit and as part of the child's introduction into the culture of his or her home. But we need to know what we are doing and why.

Our Christian faith is firmly founded on the resurrection of our Lord Jesus Christ. This is the absolute which has never been the subject of any heresy. St Paul tells the Corinthians quite unequivocally:

> . . . if Christ has not been raised then our preaching is useless and your believing it is useless.[4]

Thus it is the resurrection of Christ and his presence with us *in the Spirit* now and until the end of time, that is at the core of our Christian faith. The feast of Easter has priority over all the other feasts of the liturgical year and should be celebrated with great joy and festivity.

In the northern hemisphere Easter coincides with the springtide of the year which provides an opportunity for the house to be made joyful with growing things such as catkins, bulbs and flowers. These living, growing things, along with a lighted candle, are powerful symbols of Christ as Life and Light. We might garland the cross or make an Easter garden and put over them the opening line of the Mass for Easter Sunday: 'I am risen and am still with you.'

I have never lived in the southern hemisphere but I am

sure that a lighted candle, along with the rich colours of late summer brought into the home would form a fitting symbol of the glorified, risen Christ. Wherever we live, we will celebrate in the silence of our meditation, the intimate presence of Jesus who died and who now lives for ever as the risen Christ and Lord of all.

Our three-and-four-year olds will be ready to hear the story of the Resurrection and I would advocate telling it very beautifully through one of the apparitions. The appearance to Mary Magdalene in the garden is a particularly lovely way of introducing the risen Christ. He is different yet the same. He is with us now in a way which is different from the way he was before he died, but it is the same Jesus who is now and for always. We close our eyes so as to help us stop thinking about other things and just BE with him saying his name to ourselves. This is the beginning of meditation with a mantra. The same story could be told over and over again all through the Easter season, always leading into a few minutes of silence in the presence of Jesus.

The Christmas story also needs to be retold in the same way, but we should bear in mind that, whereas the Easter Jesus, the Risen Christ, is a present reality, the Babe of Bethlehem is a part of history. Jesus is no longer a baby; he is, and always will be, the Risen Lord.

The Christmas celebration of the mystery of the Incarnation finds its completion and fulfilment in the celebration of the death and resurrection of Jesus in the Easter cycle. The coming of Jesus into the world is worthy of celebration indeed but let us keep it in proportion.

Children readily understand that the adults around them celebrate their birthdays, and so it is fitting that we celebrate the birthday of Jesus with a special meal and presents. A visit to the crib, either in the home or in church, is part of that celebration. It was St Francis of Assisi who, in his childlike piety, had the idea of enacting the nativity scene with a crib in order to arouse the devotion of his brothers and friends. The crib was primarily to help adults reflect on the mystery of the Incarnation, and children will participate in it through the sincerity and devotion of their adults.

The Christmas story receives its validity from the fact that this Jesus who was born in Bethlehem, died on the cross, was raised to life again and now lives as Lord of all creation. In St Paul's famous passage in the Letter to the Philippians, we read that:

His state was divine
yet he did not cling
to his equality with God
but emptied himself
to assume the condition of a slave,
and became as men are;   HE WAS BORN
and being as all men are,
he was humbler yet,
even to accepting death,   DIED
death on a cross.
But God raised him high   WAS RAISED TO LIFE
and gave him the name
which is above all other names
so that all beings
in the heavens, on earth   AS
and in the underworld   LORD
should bend the knee   OF ALL
at the name of Jesus   CREATION
and that every tongue should acclaim
    JESUS CHRIST AS LORD
to the glory of God the Father.[5]

7

Scripture, Story-telling and Meditation

It is the intelligent guess of the archaeologists who ponder these things, that story-telling began at the time when early humans discovered fire and learnt to control it. These hunters and gatherers would obviously have been very busy during daylight hours, searching for food. But after dark there would have been much to recount about their hunting exploits and their adventures in the forest, as they ate their meal in the glow and warmth of the fire. Twenty to 25 appears to have been a constant size for the groups, a good number for the spinning of yarns. These stories were told over and over, and were added to as time passed.

The urge towards communication through story-telling is deeply implanted in the human psyche, an urge finding a natural expression in dramatic presentation through body language and the use of the senses. Modern Anglo-Saxon society has, for the most part, withdrawn into a culture of understatement and a negation of spontaneous expression in story-telling. Our children are the losers; they need to be involved, with their teacher in a relaxed, intimate situation, away from the daily hubbub of life.

Not unnaturally, perhaps, we tend to think of Jesus delivering his teaching somewhat in the style of a modern-day sermon. But we are told that the ordinary people followed in their hundreds to hear him and that he held them spellbound. Following the custom of the time, he would have used his whole person to communicate with his audience, making them laugh, making them cry, getting them to respond to his questions. His stories would have been so colourfully and dynamically presented that the people would have talked about them at home and retold them to their children.

The involvement of our children needs to be such that they call for the same story over and over again. And this is excellent because in this way it will penetrate their consciousness at a deep and permanent level. They will come to love it so much that they will recount it to the other grown-ups close to them and to themselves while lying in bed before going to sleep.

Not only do we need to tell the stories as stories about Jesus, or stories that Jesus told, but our set purpose must be to help the children build up a loving relationship with Jesus *in the flesh*[1] and bring them to this same Jesus, present with us now *in the Spirit*. Some suggestions about how to do this are given further on in this chapter.

If you are a natural story-teller use all your skills and abilities. If you feel less sure of yourself, take a bit of time to think about the medium through which you express yourself most easily; this will be the one to build on in your story-telling. Put another way, what moves you most? Is it beauty or music? Literature, art or drama? Science or the great outdoors? Somewhere inside you is a key to good story-telling and, if you can find it, it will liberate you as well as the children in your care. In the present context, that of meditation, it can lead both you and them into the silence of *pure prayer*.

When preparing to tell the story, the teacher will first ponder the Gospel accounts and rehearse the talk he/she proposes to give, remembering that the purpose is to prepare the way for those few moments of *being with* the same Jesus who was in that story and is still with us now.

The importance of experiencing the Gospel stories and the sayings of Jesus is very great for us all. We need to have what St Thomas Aquinas calls 'many memories' of Jesus if we are to build up a deep, enduring relationship with him. 'Experience is the fruit of many memories', said St Thomas. This is doubly important during the years of childhood. Thought should be given to ways in which the experience can be deepened for this particular child or group of children. Here are some examples of how lessons might be developed along the above lines.

THE UNDER SEVENS

The calming of the storm on the lake
Matthew 19:13, Mark 10:15, Luke 18:15

I suggest that the teacher, whether in or out of school, would do well to ponder all the accounts in preparing the story. Mark, for example, tells that Jesus was asleep with his head on a cushion, a detail which little children will relish. Bearing in mind that they are still very dependent on their relationships with adults, we will help them to relate to Jesus as someone with whom they feel safe and at home, so that the culmination of the story will be in the words of Jesus to his terrified apostles: 'Why are you frightened? I am with you.' This last phrase is implicit in the words about lack of faith as reported in all three Gospels. It also expresses the essence of the Incarnation: Jesus with us. The children will be *experiencing* the Incarnation without the word actually being used. This will come later, as also will a further understanding that the oneness of Jesus with God is to be learnt through his power over the forces of nature.

I once witnessed a lesson given to four-and-a-half and five-year olds by someone who loved music, but other media could equally well be employed. This particular teacher had recorded on tape a short passage from the storm in Mendelssohn's 'Fingal's Cave', which was played after she had described the storm on the sea of Galilee. A peaceful piano passage from Liszt accompanied the ending of the story. The children were so involved that one could hear little voices behind the music saying: 'Terrible storm' and 'All quiet!' The quiet music reinforced the impact of the peace brought by Jesus when the waters were stilled, and prepared the children for the culminating moments of *being with* Jesus, just saying his name four or five times, silently, in their heart, with eyes closed.

I suggest that they say the word 'in their heart' rather than that they spend time with 'Jesus living in their heart'. Children of this age think in a concrete, literal way and all too easily conjure up Jesus as a little man curled up inside their physical heart! Equally to be avoided with such young children is talking about Jesus being everywhere. They can but take this in a crude sense because of their stage of mental development, and it leads to nonsense questions such as: 'Is he under the table? In the teapot? Sitting on top of the cupboard?' This applies equally to their being told that Jesus is in the tabernacle. Adults have confessed to thinking of him as a little gingerbread man sitting there in the dark feeling lonely. What a travesty of the fundamental Christian belief in the risen, glorified Christ!

Explanations are out of place at this age. Things are either true in a concrete sense or are magical in the children's way of thinking and neither gives the right answer to the presence of Jesus. Growth comes through identification with a caring adult. Faith is communicated by faith.

Jesus with little children
Matthew 9:20, Mark 1:29, Luke 8:43

Again, the aim will be to build up a relationship with Jesus who is shown in the story talking with children just like them. He is happy to be with them and they are very happy to be with him. Some may be talking to him, telling him secrets, while others may be content just to be in his company without saying anything.

This particular Gospel passage lends itself very well to a pictorial representation. This might be built up by the teacher as the story progresses, each child being made real as he/she appears in the picture. It need not be a masterpiece; children are very tolerant! Or a picture from a religious book could be enlarged for the purpose. Always, the lesson leads to those few moments of *being with* Jesus now.

The healing of Jairus' daughter
Matthew 9:18, Mark 5:21, Luke 8:40

A graphic story is built up from the angle of Jairus himself: his distress and worry at home, his request to Jesus and his anxiety when Jesus delays in order to cure the woman in the crowd. (This incident could form a story on its own but here it is just mentioned as a worrying interruption for Jairus.) Jesus says to him, and later to his wife and the mourners: 'Don't worry – I'm here.' As in the story of the calming of the storm, it is implied in the Gospel text: 'Do not be afraid: only have faith.'

This very dramatic story lends itself well to being acted out by a group of six-year-olds. As in the first story, there is a wonderfully dramatic juxtaposition of fear and peace as the anxiety of Jairus and the noise of the wailing mourners and musicians, give way to utter stupefaction as they are 'overcome with astonishment' at the loving power of Jesus. The children can experience these two states by acting out or by dancing the story. Through whatever medium, the children come through to the silence that leads to the short period of meditation using the name of Jesus as a mantra.

The woman with the issue of blood
Matthew 9:20, Mark 5:25, Luke 8:43

This could be a very quiet, intimate talk about a woman who had been ill for a long time but didn't want everybody to know about it. She felt sure that if she could only touch Jesus, his loving power would make her better. We tell how this same Jesus died on the cross and rose again. He has told us that he is now always with us, even to the end of the world. We tell him about our troubles and then stay with him, content just to *be with* him saying his name.

The healing of Peter's mother-in-law
Matthew 8:14, Mark 1:29, Luke 4:38

Peter brings Jesus and his friends to his home for a meal after Jesus has been working all day teaching crowds of people about God our Father. They find that Granny is ill and they ask Jesus to help her. He goes over to her at once and, with great love, puts his hand on her forehead to soothe her and straight away she feels better and gets up to prepare the meal for everyone.

We do not speak of it as a miracle. We only want to show that Jesus is kind and loving to her, and, by implication, to us. He is that sort of person. Children will be able to relate to this kindness if they have experienced it themselves when they have been in bed with a temperature and their mother has placed a cool hand on their forehead which has made them feel better.

Once again, let me say that this lesson needs to be fleshed out so that it may be assimilated by the children at the centre of their being, leading to those few moments of meditation, of *being with* Jesus present with us now. By the age of six, most children will be able to sustain five minutes of silent repetition of the name Jesus without any strain.

The main things to be borne in mind when telling stories to children who have not reached the age of reason are:

1 Tell actual stories about Jesus himself with the sole aim of leading the children into a relationship with him.
2 Jesus needs to be seen as a strong, loving person who is understanding and with whom one is safe.

SEVEN TO NINE YEAR OLDS

These ages are, of course, relative, as some children mature earlier than others and some later. The period I intend to cover in this section is from the time a child can distinguish between fact and fantasy, which normally happens between six and seven-and-a-half, up to around the age of nine or ten. All growth takes place through alternating periods of energy and rest, and the transition to rational thinking is no exception. This stage is sometimes called 'the threshold of conscience'. On a Monday a child may appear to have a firm grasp of the difference between what is based in reality and what is not, while on the Tuesday he/she may revert to a four-year-old's way of thinking. Up to now the children will have learnt about Jesus exclusively through their relationship with an adult, and it is therefore vitally important that the relationship be loving and warm. Though a loving relationship will always remain the key factor in passing on our Christian faith to the next generation, other factors now enter in.

This one-to-one relationship begins to broaden out and children form relationships and pursue interests outside the immediate family circle. They begin to ask *why* this or that is to be done, not from petulance but because they want to know the reason; they are no longer content to do things just because 'Mummy says so'. They tend to be more reserved about their wrong-doings, a reserve which must be respected. It is not advisable, once this stage has been reached, for a mother to try to keep her child dependent upon her to the extent of telling her everything that has happened, for good or bad, during the day. We must not put ourselves between God and a child either by keeping him/her in subjection to us or by making ourselves appear indispensable.

At this time, too, children may begin to pray on their own just because they want to and not from any outside pressure or desire to please. Let the adult accept it without comment. All this calls for great tact and selflessness, but this selflessness is, in itself, a lesson which will be picked up, maybe only subconsciously, by the children.

Our emphasis in the telling of Gospel stories will change. Up till this time we have been endeavouring to build up a personal relationship with Jesus whom the child would see as an ideal parent. It is time now to widen this view and to discover that love calls for a response. Stories such as the call of Matthew,[2] of the four fishermen by the lakeside,[3] and of the two disciples of John the Baptist[4] appeal to the children's generosity and will give a new dimension to their time of *being with* Jesus as the climax of each lesson. These dynamic stories lend themselves to many forms of expression, and the children will now be capable of taking a greater part in the preparation and execution of whatever medium is being used.

They watch Jesus as he goes about healing and teaching.[5] They begin to relate to him as a friend and try to imitate him.

In the Roman Catholic Church this is also the time for preparing children for their First Communion which makes it an ideal period for leading children towards an experienced understanding that love calls for a response of love. Holy Communion can be introduced as an extra special way of loving within an already existing relationship. You only give a hug to someone you already know and love; it brings an extra closeness. So in Holy Communion our relationship of love with Jesus is celebrated and deepened and this calls for a response of love.

In Holy Communion we make our response to the self-giving of Jesus at the Last Supper with our own self-giving to Jesus in love. This is the culmination and resolution of every celebration of the Eucharist. On their First Communion day the children enter into this special dialogue of love. As their life unfolds they will understand ever more fully the meaning of the suffering which is involved in self-giving. This is the mystery of death and resurrection, of life arising from death, being worked out in our own lives.

After Holy Communion we spend a little time just content to *be with* Jesus saying his name lovingly. This is our time of meditation. After that we can talk to him about our interests and pray for our friends and our needs.[6]

When the children have definitively crossed over the 'threshold of conscience' they will be ready for a further understanding of prayer.

In Luke 9:18 we read that 'he was praying alone in the presence of his disciples'. This could be discussed and also related to our own prayer. Many children are afraid of being physically alone and, using this text, we can help a child to realize that one can 'go by oneself' while remaining in company. This is indeed a very fruitful and supportive way of praying. A great many adults who meditate regularly in their own lives find the courage to persevere by meeting in a group locally on a weekly basis.

Jesus called God *Father* and sometimes *Abba*, which was a word for use within the family and which could be translated as 'dear Father'. He taught us to do the same. This might be a good time in the children's education in Christian prayer to lead them towards praying to the Father with Jesus. Again, this will be done experientially and no dogmas will be formulated. It will be of inestimable value to children, both now and in later life, if we are able to help them form the habit of praying in this way. Perhaps, if we find it difficult ourselves, it is because no one did this for us.

The more one ponders the Gospels the clearer it becomes that the desire of Jesus is to draw us to himself in order that, with him, we may go to the Father in trustful, child-like love and self-giving. The children will already have an experience of Jesus through the Gospel stories they know so well by now. They have seen that he is essentially *loving, caring* and *forgiving*.

Basing one's teaching on John 14:7, 'If you know me, you know my Father too', I suggest that the children be led to look at Jesus in a situation where he is being particularly *loving*, as for example in the blessing of little children,[7] and then juxtapose this with the story about the lost sheep which ends with Jesus saying: 'Your Father in heaven never wants any of these little ones to be lost.'[8] In this way Jesus and the Father are seen as one in that they are both *loving*.

Similarly, we can go over one of the many stories where Jesus is shown as *caring*, and from that listen to him telling us about how no sparrow falls to the ground without our Father knowing and how there is no need to be afraid because we are worth more than hundreds of sparrows.[9] In this way Jesus and the Father are seen as one in that they are both *caring*.

Then again, we take one of the stories that the children know about Jesus being *forgiving*, and then listen to Jesus telling us: 'Yes, if you forgive others their failings, your heavenly Father will forgive you yours. . . .'[10] In this story, both Jesus and the Father are seen to be one in *forgiving*.

Following on lessons such as the above which deal with the theme of Jesus and the Father being one in the way they act, the children are led to look at the prayer of Jesus himself. Luke is at pains to show us how central personal prayer was to Jesus in his everyday life.[11] In his prayer time Jesus was *being with* God our Father in the same way that we spend time *being with* Jesus in our meditation time. We know from the Gospels that Jesus used the word *Abba*, dear Father, in his prayer. This is the time to suggest to the children that they might like to change their prayer word from *Jesus* to *Abba* so as to pray with Jesus to God our Father.

By the time the children are eight or nine years old some of them, at least, will have established a pattern of meditation apart from the lesson time. They could be encouraged to put aside specific times each day, perhaps after dressing in the morning and last thing at night.

TEN TO TWELVE YEAR OLDS

Now is the time for telling and discussing the parables. If taken earlier, most children will only be able to accept them as literal stories which Jesus told and not as a teaching technique for putting over a point. For example, younger children will be glad that the woman who lost her coin has found it and has called in her neighbours to rejoice with her, but will not be able to make the mental shift which is needed to realize that the woman represents God being concerned about sinners and rejoicing when they repent.

The Psalms relating to the greatness of God and his creation have a grand ring about them which appeals to this age of child and parts of them could easily be learnt by heart. The sheer poetry of Psalms 8 and 18 will captivate a ten-year-old, and those towards the end of the Psalter are particularly apt for this age group. I would mention specifically parts of Psalm 136 and 139 and from 145 onwards. Children and adults alike can make their own psalms of praise, modelled on these yet relating to their immediate situation. 'How I thank you, God, for the smashing sound of motorbikes!' was one boy's heartfelt prayer of praise, pasted into the Book of Psalms his class was compiling.

Meditation should now become more and more each child's own responsibility. Daily periods of meditation in the home give the best teaching now even if the child does not join in or give any indication of being aware that meditation is happening in the house. In some schools it may be possible to have a voluntary period of meditation at some point during the day.

Children of twelve are at the pivotal point between child-hood and adolescence, and may well manifest an ambiv-alence comparable to that at the threshold of conscience period. They may continue with their meditation at times and not at others; this is all in the nature of growing up, but the seed has been sown over the years of childhood and we need not be alarmed if it all seems to have come to nothing. It is deep within and may lie dormant for a very long time. The active involvement of parents in introducing their children to meditation will now be minimal, but let them be assured that their own example, even if it appears to be ignored, is enormously powerful. The only injurious thing would be to nag or otherwise make the child or young person feel that he/she is a disappointment to them. Be endlessly full of hope and love just as the Lord God is. Remember, he has their good at heart even more deeply than you have, as this blessing from the Book of Numbers shows:

> The Lord bless you
>   and keep you.
> The Lord make his light
>   shine upon you.
> The Lord turn his face towards you
>   and give you peace.

8

Jesus at Home

Jesus was born into a Jewish family of the House of David, during the period of the Roman occupation of Palestine. What kind of culture was he born into? And how did this affect his life and teaching? In this chapter we look at his formative years, then at the way he taught. Then, in Chapter 9, we consider how the first teachers in the Early Church passed on the message they had received from him. Looking in this way at our Christian roots, we will find enlightenment regarding our own involvement in the passing on of the Christian tradition.

Jesus was brought up in a devout family, in close contact with many of his relations. The current nuclear family had not been conceived of in those days, and thus the Holy Family, far from living a secluded life on their own, would almost certainly have been part of an extended family group. The brothers of the Lord, whom we hear of during the public life of Jesus, would all have been part of this extended family.

We know that Joseph was a carpenter, which was a much respected trade and one that would have brought him into contact with the townspeople and farmers of the area, occasioning a constant flux of comings and goings in the home. Jesus was part of all this busy life and, except for his early childhood when he was in the care of his mother, he would have been the constant companion of Joseph.

The boys of the family learnt their religion, their trade and all they knew from their father.

It is interesting, in this context, to hear Jesus saying: 'The Son can do nothing by himself, he can do only what he sees the Father doing: and whatever the Father does the Son does too.'[1] This saying has its roots in an ancient proverb used by craftsmen: 'The son does nothing except what he sees his father doing.' The loving father is eager to pass on his craft to his son, and the son is eager to learn.

The amount of time given to prayer by the household, would, by modern Western standards, have been considered very long. The *Shema* was the main part of the daily home liturgy and was recited morning and evening. It is the solemn proclamation that God is One, and that we have a duty to love him and obey him. It also stresses the duty – of particular note to us – of instructing the children in this same teaching, so that, through them, it may be handed down for ever. The *Shema* consists of three prayers from the Torah.[2] Here is the part which includes the passage concerning the importance of teaching it to children:

Listen, Israel: Yahweh our God is the one Yahweh. You shall love Yahweh your God with all your heart, with all your soul, with all your strength. Let these words I urge on you today be written on your heart. *You shall repeat them to your children and say them over to them whether at rest in your house or walking abroad, at your lying down or at your rising.*

This teaching of loving the One God with one's whole heart, soul and strength, which Jesus had repeated morning and evening from the age of twelve, became the cornerstone of his own teaching, and it was most certainly his intention that it should be handed on from generation to generation, from parent to child, from teacher to taught.

71

Now it is the turn of our generation to pass on to our children this core teaching of the Jewish faith which we, as Christians, have inherited through Jesus.

The part of the *Shema* recorded above was to be repeated over and over during the day. It is a form of what we now call a mantra.

It was within the religious atmosphere of the home, and particularly through such repetition of the sacred texts that Jesus 'increased in wisdom, in stature, and in favour with God and men'.[3] Though not recorded in the Gospels, we can be certain that Jesus also loved to pray alone as a child and as a young man. We know he had established a habit of praying alone at night by the time he came to his public life. We read of an occasion when, after saying goodbye to the crowds, he went off into the hills to pray.[4] At another time we are told that he spent the whole night in prayer to God.[5] And Mark tells us that very early one morning, long before daylight, Jesus got up, left the house, and went out of the town to a lonely place where he prayed. When Peter and his companions discovered he was missing, they went off in search of him, and we learn that they found him in his lonely place and, in some exasperation it would seem, exclaimed: 'Everybody is looking for you.'[6]

When we and our children meditate we withdraw from our activities for this short period to attend solely to the presence and love of God in the silence of faith, just as Jesus did. This twice daily practice throughout childhood offers a powerful formative influence which, in conjunction with the benefits of a Christian home and an intelligent use of Scripture, constitute an ideal Christian formation.

The Sabbath was for the Jews, and of course still is, the supremely holy day which celebrated the creation of the world. No work was done on the Sabbath. In the peaceful and harmonious atmosphere of the home the mother lit two candles as it began at sundown on the Friday, and recited the blessing: 'Blessed are you, O Lord our God, King of all the world, who made us holy with your laws, and commanded us to kindle the Sabbath lights.' This lighting of the candles, which is the responsibility of the mother, emphasizes the woman's fundamental importance in the family; it is she who lights the fire in the hearth and who is the source of light that gives her family peace and joy in a special way on the holy day of the Lord. Mothers! You have a wonderful role to fulfil in your home.

Another important way in which the children learnt their religion was through family participation in the great festivals. These festivals provided a multi-media presentation of the sacred events. The three pilgrim feasts commemorated God's care of the Jews at the time of the Exodus. All the people left their work and went up to Jerusalem to celebrate physically as well as spiritually the fact that they were a pilgrim people. The spring festival of the Pasch relived the story of God's saving power in delivering his People from the hands of Pharoah. This was retold every year by the head of the family after he had been asked by the youngest child, in a ritual question, to do so. The autumn festival, the feast of Tabernacles, commemorated the tents set up in the desert during the 40 years that the Jews dwelt there before entering the Promised Land. The people built tents of leafy branches and lived in them for the period of the feast, and through this active participation in the heart of their family, the children learnt about their sacred history which revealed the unfailing loving kindness of God.

Thus the children's religious education began in the home through the imitation of their parents and within a whole way of life celebrating what God had done and was still doing for them.

When they grew older the boys were entrusted to a

teacher at whose feet they sat to learn the Law by heart. The teacher became a very important influence in every boy's life. The girls stayed with their mothers! When the boys reached adulthood they would choose a teacher, mostly from among the Pharisees or the Essenes, to continue their learning. We know that Peter, Andrew, Philip and Nathanael continued their education with John the Baptist until they left him to become followers of Jesus.

Jesus is called 'teacher' some 48 times in the Gospels, and although he taught mostly in the synagogue, he also taught in the open air, on the hillside and by the lakeside in Galilee. He had a peripatetic school, his students following him wherever he went. With time there came to be an inner group who remained constantly in his company, working with him, adopting his way of life and absorbing his teaching. Theirs was not a merely passive role; they became active collaborators in the mission of Jesus.

It was customary for young men to choose their own teacher. It is very interesting to note that Jesus reversed this practice: 'You did not choose me; I chose you',[7] and also: 'Then Jesus went up a hill and called to himself the men he wanted. They came to him, and he chose twelve, whom he named apostles. "I have chosen you to be with me" he told them.'[8] This gives us pause for thought. It is Jesus who has chosen us to be with him: this is our primary call.

The other practice he reversed was that of the students paying for tuition by acts of service to their master. 'I am among you as one who serves',[9] expresses his whole attitude to others. He taught his followers that they were to serve others even as he did. They were to be active collaborators in his mission. This attitude of selfless service is the hallmark of a true follower of Jesus.

The ministry of Jesus is dominated by an initiative-taking which is quite different from the way of the Pharisees and the Essenes. They saw their role as passing on the Law of Moses, while Jesus receives his inspiration (spirit) from his Father. He heals on the Sabbath because he is doing no more than his Father: 'My Father goes on working and so do I.'[10] He sees evidence of his Father's attitude through looking at nature:

> You have learnt how it was said: *You must love your neighbour* and hate your enemy. But I say this to you: love your enemies and pray for those who persecute you; in this way you will be sons of your Father in heaven, for he causes his sun to rise on bad men as well as good, and his rain to fall on honest and dishonest men alike. You must therefore be perfect just as your heavenly Father is perfect.[11]

Like his Father, Jesus also pursues this way of positive and all-inclusive goodness. Nature shows him a God of universal love. In calling himself the Good Shepherd, for example, he is modelling himself on God as portrayed in Ezekiel Chapter 34.

He is not like a human shepherd, even the best of them, because the human shepherd cares for his sheep primarily for what the sheep can give him: money, meat, wool or milk. The total concern of his Father is for the sheep themselves. Jesus went, with total concern, to the physically and mentally sick, the lepers, the lame, the blind, the tax collectors and sinners, and which of us is not in that group?

There was a freshness and creativity in his way of teaching. People were spellbound by his words.[12] Luke reports that they were all filled with amazement, *ekstasis*.[13] Jesus is not a memory-expert constantly drilling lessons into his pupils. He does not lecture from prepared notes; his address is spontaneous, fresh; he speaks to people in their present concrete situations. He uses his whole being in telling his stories, acting them out, dancing. This would have been normal in a good teacher, and he was certainly that. 'He adjusted to his people's way of talking and to their pattern of thought. And he spoke out of the predicament of their time.'[14]

He spoke in the familiar surroundings of a home, a small synagogue, a boat, the seashore, anywhere that he found people ready to listen. He entered into dialogue with them. This creativity of Jesus' teaching was something contagious that the apostles caught from him through continuous contact over three years, and it was this creative word of God that was carried by them into the wider world after his resurrection. Jesus wrote no words or compendium of teaching; the Good News was to travel from person to person through enthusiastic, live communicators. We are the direct heirs of this vibrant message to be passed on from generation to generation.

9

Jesus and the Church

In the Early Church the office of teacher was much respected, being ranked third after apostles and prophets. But at the same time there was a strong fear of human discipleship. A Christian was to be a disciple of no man but of Christ himself.

So the teacher in the Early Church, though very important, is to be humble, hidden, part of ordinary Christian life. He is to teach primarily through example, leading his converts into a whole new way of life, one modelled on the life of Jesus himself, in preparation for their baptism. His principal concerns were to show how Jesus fulfilled the Scriptures, and to hand on the living tradition of Jesus which was embodied in the life of the teacher within the group of believers. The most important part of the learning process was imitation of the teacher, and then interaction with the local group and the larger community. The New Testament view of the teacher's role was non-academic: he was teaching a new Way of life through his own example of commitment to it.

The Spirit at work in the teacher's life enabling him to represent Jesus faithfully to others was the beginning of the apostolic tradition. The creativity and spontaneity produced in Jesus by the Spirit produced the same creativity and spontaneity in the teacher. The children were all part of this learning, their parents being their teachers. The codification of the teaching would have a necessary place in later centuries, but with it came the danger of the teaching being considered as a separate body of knowledge, replacing the learning through the living tradition embodied in the teacher and the community. This aberration is not infrequently expressed nowadays in sentiments such as: 'I've no use for religion myself but I would like my children to know about it.'

The First Letter to the Thessalonians, which was written only some fifteen to twenty years after the death and resurrection of Jesus, is probably the earliest Christian document we possess. In it Paul states that the first Christians learned their new way of life by imitating the 'little church' composed of Paul and his companions. He says to them: 'Take me for your model, as I take Christ',[1] meaning that they are to model themselves on the life of Christ as exemplified in Paul and his companions. This is what Paul sees as apostolic tradition. His criterion for a true apostle (teacher) is a manner of life completely dedicated to others even when this entails intense suffering and heroic personal sacrifice. Paul sees his life as a mediating link between Jesus and the new churches. He says to the Thessalonians: 'You were led to become imitators of us, and of the Lord; and it was with the joy of the Holy Spirit that you took to the gospel, in spite of the great opposition all around you.'[2]

Jesus, and Paul after him, have given us the ideal. But from the time of Jesus' own life on earth human frailty has been strongly present. After three years in his intimate company, Jesus found the disciples talking among themselves about which of them should be the greatest. On another occasion he sounded frustrated with their slowness to learn: 'Do you not yet understand? Have you no perception? Are your minds closed? Have you eyes that do not see, ears that do not hear? Or do you not remember?'[3]

On one occasion Jesus told a parable about the wheat and the weeds growing up together till harvest time, 'and not till then will they be separated'.[4] This message can be applied to the Way of Jesus from the time when Jesus was teaching the apostles himself, through the Early Church and every succeeding generation, to our own times, our own lives, and to the end of the world. So let us have no worries about our inadequacies and failures. He will nurture the wheat even though we may only be aware of the weeds in our lives and teaching, and in the wider Christian community.

For this reason not everything in the Early Church is to be taken on board by us, the weeds are there as well as the wheat. Many of the early Christian communities took a negative attitude to the world about them, in contrast to Jesus who drew much of his teaching from acute observation and sensitivity to God's work in history and in the world of nature. There developed a tendency in some sectors of the Church to regard human nature itself with undue pessimism. This was due in part to the influence of Greek philosophy which regarded the human body as a corrupt vessel containing a noble soul: despite the influence of the Spirit, the human element was always present. Also the teaching was decidedly paternalistic, the importance of exact obedience being stressed often at the expense of stifling individual creativity and personal decision. This led to a lack of dialogue and spontaneity. It is now obvious to us all that these weeds are still with us in the Church and in our persons today. Having acknowledged this, let us focus our efforts on cultivating the wheat as far as we are able.

Our children will be led to the imitation and following of Christ through example and influence. The intuitive, feminine side needs to be developed to counter-balance the masculine element in teaching. This relates back once more to the dual root of the word education and means the assimilation of a lifestyle from those who are already living it, just as it did in the beginning of the Church. The living tradition about Jesus is embodied, now as then, in the lives of people who are following in the Way themselves, however haltingly. This is a Way of life based on love: 'You shall love your God with your heart, soul and strength.'

The apostles had no textbook, but they accompanied Jesus as he went about his daily life. As Jesus' source material was the Old Testament, from where he learnt of the great works of God for his People through their history and through the wonders of the natural world, so our source material is likewise found in the Scriptures and in the study of God's wonderful acts in the universe. Here there is no distinction between teaching prayer and teaching religion. They form one inseparable whole as they did in the consciousness of Jesus himself. Every lesson we teach must be a prayer, and every prayer a personal encounter with God through Jesus.

CHILDREN

Your children are not your children.
They are the sons and daughters of Life's longing for
    itself.
They come through you, but not from you,
And though they are with you, yet they belong not to
    you.
You may give them your love, but not your thoughts,
For they have their own thoughts.
You may house their bodies, but not their souls.
For their souls dwell in the house of tomorrow,
which you cannot visit, not even in your dreams.
You may strive to be like them, but seek not to make them
    like you.

For life goes not backwards, nor tarries with yesterday.
You are the bows from which your children as living
    arrows are sent forth.
The Archer sees the mark upon the path of the infinite
    and He bends you with His might,
So that His arrows may go swift and far.

Let your bending in the Archer's hand be for gladness.
For even as He loves the arrow that flies,
So He loves also the bow that is stable.

Kahlil Gibran, The Prophet, Pan Books

Notes

Introduction

1 *Saccidananda*, Henri Le Saux. ISPCK, PO Box 1585, Kashmere Gate, Delhi 110 006.
2 1 Cor. 1:23–25 (Jerusalem Bible, as are all the Scriptural quotations unless otherwise stated).
3 1 Cor. 2:4–5.

Chapter 1   The Pedigree of Christian Mantra Meditation

1 From the Latin *mederi* originally, to attend to, *meditari* to apply oneself to, to study, to reflect upon. Eric Partridge, *Origins. A Short Etymological Dictionary of Modern English*. Routledge and Kegan Paul, 4th ed, 1966.
2 *A Book of Peace. Children's Art Through Meditation*. Published in Germany. Available in England from the International Centre for Future Education, P.O. Box 927, London NW1 6SS.
3 *Meditation for Children*. University of the Trees, P.O. Box 66, Boulder Creek, CA 95006.
4 John Cassian, trans. Colm Luibheid, *Classics of Western Spirituality*. Paulist Press.
5 Writings from the *Philokalia* on Prayer of the Heart, p. 33.
6 *The Cloud of Unknowing and Other Works*, trans. Clifton Wolters. Penguin Classics.
7 *Spiritual Exercises of St Ignatius*, ed. L. Puhl sj, pp. 110–112.
8 St Ignatius College, Stamford Hill, London, England.
9 cf. Ch. 5, Neil McKenty, *In the Stillness Dancing. The Journey of John Main*. Darton, Longman and Todd.

10 John Main, 'Christian Meditation', *The Gethsemane Talks*, p. 11.
11 Chanodya Upanishad, 3:14, trans. Mascaro.
12 Quoted in *In the Stillness Dancing, op. cit.*, p. 51.
13 A frequently updated *International Directory of Meditation Groups* is available from Medio Media Ltd., 23 Kensington Square, London W8 5HN.
14 Eric Partridge, *op. cit.*
15 Exodus 3:5.
16 John 4:14.
17 Raymond B. Blakney, *Meister Eckhart. A Modern Translation*. Harper and Row 1941.
18 Theresa O'Callaghan Scheihing with Louis M. Savary, *Our Treasured Heritage. Teaching Christian Meditation to Children*, p. 22. Crossroad.
19 John Main, *Community of Love*. Darton, Longman and Todd. Available from Medio Media Ltd.

Chapter 2   The Way to Teach or To Teach the Way

1 Eph. 2:18.
2 John 1:39 and Luke 9:59.
3 John 14:6.
4 John 14:9.
5 1 Cor. 4:15ff.
6 Col. 3:16, *Good News Version*.
7 2 Cor. 12:9, *Good News Version*.
8 *Lots of Love*. A collection of children's sayings compiled by Nanette Newman. William Collins 1974.
9 1 Cor. 16:22–24.
10 Rev. 22:17, 20–21.
11 Quoted in Louis Bouyer, *The Spirituality of The New Testament and The Fathers*. Burns Oates, English trans. 1963.
12 *The Cloud of Unknowing and Other Works*, trans. Clifton Wolters. Penguin Classics.

Chapter 3   The First Years

1 With the exception of the last, which is anonymous, the following quotes are from Edward Robinson, *The Original Vision:*

A Study of the Religious Experience of Childhood. The Seabury Press 1983.
2 *Ibid*.

Chapter 4   The Home

1 *Retractions*, I (viii) 3, (Migne PL XXXII).
2 Ben Okri, *The Famished Road*. Jonathan Cape 1991.
3 Kevin Kelley, *The Home Planet: Images and Reflections of Earth from Space Explorers*. Queen Anne Press 1988.

Chapter 5   The Fostering of Wonder

1 Discourse of John Paul II to participants of the National Congress of the Italian Association of Catholic Teachers, 6 December 1984. Reported in translation in *l'Osservatore Romano*, 14 January 1985.
2 Benedikt Taschen, *Henri Matisse*, edited and produced Walther, trans. Michael Halse. Verlay GmbH and Co.
3 *Pablo Picasso, ibid*.
4 *Marc Chagall, ibid*.
5 *Henri Matisse, ibid*.
6 Quoted in Duncan Robinson, *Stanley Spencer*. Phaidon.
7 *Ibid*.
8 Nanette Newman, *Lots of Love*. William Collins 1979.
9 Cf. Matt. 11:25.
10 Quoted in Francis Huxley, *The Way of the Sacred*. Bloomsbury Books.
11 John Cassian, Conference 10:14, *The Classics of Western Spirituality*. Paulist Press.
12 Thomas Berry, *Dream of the Earth*. Sierra Club 1988.
13 Brian Swimme, *The Universe is a Green Dragon: A Cosmic Creation Story*. Bear & Co.
14 'Canticle to the Cosmos', video in 12 parts. New Story Project, 134 Coleen St., Livermore, CA 94550. As yet not available in Europe.
15 *Earthspirit: A Handbook for Nurturing an Ecological Christianity*. Twenty-Third Publications.
16 Sankey, Sullivan and Watson, *At Home on Planet Earth: An Integrated Course in Science and Religion*. Basil Blackwell 1988.

17 Kevin Kelly, *The Home Planet*. Queen Anne Press 1988.
18 Brian Swimme, *Canticle to the Cosmos Study Guide* accompanying the video series of that name. The Tides Foundation, New Story Project, 1388 Sutter St., 10th Floor, San Francisco CA 9409.

Chapter 6   The Risen Christ

1 2 Cor. 5:16.
2 I am indebted for much of the above to Hans Kung, *On Being A Christian*. Collins.
3 Matt. 28:20b.
4 1 Cor. 15:12–19.
5 Phil. 2:6–11.

Chapter 7   Scripture, Story-telling and Meditation

1 See previous chapter.
2 Matt. 9:9, Mark 2:13, Luke 5:27.
3 Matt. 4:18, Mark 1:16, Luke 5:1.
4 John 1:35.
5 Matt. 4:23, 8:14, Luke 6:17 and many others.
6 A new edition of the First Communion course, *Come to Me*, written by the author, is in preparation. To be published by McCrimmon.
7 Matt. 19:13, Mark 10:13.
8 cf. Matt. 18:13–14.
9 Matt. 10:29–31.
10 Matt. 6:14.
11 Luke 5:16, 6:12, 9:18,28–29, 11:1, 22:41.

Chapter 8   Jesus at Home

1 John 5:19.
2 Deut. 6:4–9, 11:13–21, Num. 15:37–41.
3 Luke 2:53.
4 Mark 6:46.
5 Luke 6:12.
6 Mark 1:35.
7 John 15:16.

8 Mark 3:13–15.
9 Luke 22:27.
10 John 5:17.
11 Mark 5:43.
12 Mark 1:22.
13 Luke 5:26.
14 *Pastoral Instruction on the Means of Social Communication.*

Chapter 9   Jesus and the Church

1   1 Cor. 11:1.
2   1 Thess. 1:6.
3   Mark 8:17.
4   Matt. 13:24–30.

Bibliography

*BERRY, Thomas. *Dream of the Earth* (Sierra Club Books 1988)

*BERRY, Thomas and CLARKE, Thomas. *Befriending the Earth* (Twenty-Third Publications 1991)

BAUSCH, William J. *Storytelling: Imagination and Faith* (Twenty-Third Publications 1986)

*CAMPBELL, Joseph and MOYERS, Bill. *The Power of Myth* (Doubleday 1989)

DONALDSON, Margaret. *Children's Minds* (Fontana 1988)

DONALDSON, Margaret *et al*. *Early Childhood Development* (Blackwell 1985)

*DOWD, Michael. *Earthspirit* (Twenty-Third Publications 1991)

FREEMAN, Laurence. *Light Within*. (Darton Longman and Todd 1986; Crossroad 1986)

FREEMAN, Laurence. *The Selfless Self* (DLT 1989)

*GRIFFITHS, Bede. *A New Vision of Reality* (Fount 1992)

HARRIS, Paul (ed.). *John Main by Those who Knew Him* (DLT 1991; Novalis 1991)

HARRIS, Paul. *Christian Meditation by Those who Practise It* (Dimension 1993; Novalis 1993)

KELLEY, Kevin T. *The Home Planet: Images and Reflections of Earth from Space Explorers* (Queen Anne Press 1988)

KOPCIOWSKI, Elias. *Praying with the Jewish Tradition* (SPCK 1988)

LORET, Pierre. *The Story of the Mass: From the Last Supper to the Present Day* (Redemptorist Press 1982)

MAIN, John. *Word into Silence* (DLT 1980; Paulist Press 1981)

MAIN, John *Moment of Christ* (DLT 1984; Crossroad 1984)

MAIN, John. *The Present Christ* (DLT 1985; Crossroad 1985)

MAIN, John. *The Inner Christ*. A collection of the three above works (DLT 1987)

MAIN, John. *The Way of Unknowing* (DLT 1989; Crossroad 1989)

MCKENTY, Neil. *In the Stillness Dancing: The Journey of John Main* (DLT 1986; Crossroad 1987)

MILLER, Alice. *The Drama of Being a Child* (Virago 1990)

PIERSE, Gerry. *Silence into Service* (Colomba Press 1992)

ROBINSON, Edward. *The Original Vision* (Seabury Press 1983)

*Chief SEATHL. *The Great Chief Sends Word* (1977)

SANKEY *et al*. *At Home on Planet Earth* (Blackwell 1988)

*SWIMME, Brian. *The Universe is a Green Dragon* (Bear & Co. 1984)

*SWIMME, Brian and BERRY, Thomas. *The Universe Story* (Harper Collins 1992)

*These books are available from some bookstores and from: Alan Shepherd, 14 Beckford Close, Warminster, Wilts BA12 9LW